BEYOND THE MYTHS AND MAGIC OF MENTORING

Margo Murray

with
Marna A. Owen

BEYOND THE MYTHS AND MAGIC OF MENTORING

How to Facilitate an Effective Mentoring Program

Jossey-Bass Publishers · San Francisco

BEYOND THE MYTHS AND MAGIC OF MENTORING
How to Facilitate an Effective Mentoring Program
  by Margo Murray with Marna A. Owen

Copyright © 1991 by: Jossey-Bass Inc., Publishers
                    350 Sansome Street
                    San Francisco, California 94104

Library of Congress Cataloging-in-Publication Data

Murray, Margo.
   Beyond the myths and magic of mentoring: how to facilitate an effective
mentoring program / Margo Murray with Marna A. Owen—1st ed.
      p.   cm. — (The Jossey-Bass management series)
   Includes bibliographical references.
   Includes index.
   ISBN 1-55542-333-7 (alk. paper)
   1. Mentors in business.   I. Owen, Marna A.
II. Title.   III. Series.
HF5386.M5875   1991
658.3'124—dc20
DNLM/DLC
for Library of Congress   90-25580
                                                                   CIP

 Manufactured in the United States of America on Lyons Falls Pathfinder Tradebook.
This paper is acid-free and 100 percent totally chlorine-free.

Examples from Corporate Executive Fellows, National Urban Fellows Inc.;
Eastman Kodak; Empire State College; Internal Revenue Service–Ogden
Service Center; the New York State Department of Taxation and Finance;
Rooney, Ida, Nolt and Ahern; Trinity College; Tumor Registrars
Association of California; the U.S. General Accounting Office; and Wells
Fargo Bank are used with permission.

JACKET DESIGN BY WILLI BAUM

HB Printing   10 9 8 7 6

Code 9136

The Jossey-Bass
Management Series

Consulting Editors
Human Resources

Leonard Nadler
Zeace Nadler
College Park, Maryland

Contents

ix

To my first mentor, Marcus Hanna Murray,
and to Charles Bell and Albert Ellison,
who modeled the role in facilitated processes

Preface

Mentoring has received a great deal of press coverage over the last few decades. It has been applauded as the best and criticized as the worst thing that can happen in one's career. Journal articles refer to formal mentoring programs and informal mentoring relationships in health care, universities, schools, industry, and government. Today one can find mention of mentoring in almost every publication aimed at managers, administrators, educators, human resource professionals, and the general public. The wide-ranging interest in mentoring is illustrated by the tone and content of the publications on this subject. Most of them are designed for light, almost casual reading, such as the airline-magazine stories of successful people who give credit to their mentors. Only a few serious research studies of mentoring are available; one notable example is Alleman's dissertation (1982).

Since the 1960s my clients, colleagues, and I have been systematically testing strategies for making a facilitated mentoring process work in many types of organizations in both the public and private sectors. The genesis for this facilitated mentoring model was my own experience with accelerated promotion programs in two large organizations. Each program had some of the features of mentoring, yet neither had all the components of a facilitated mentoring program. Inspired by my own good and bad mentoring experiences, and stimulated by the assessed needs of the organizations with which I worked, I developed the Facilitated Mentoring Model© and tested it in several of the line and operational functions that I managed. By early 1971 I had enough of the framework in place to use it to analyze examples from other organizations that were using some semblance of a mentoring concept (Murray-Hicks and Nugent, 1971). As the work progressed, longitudinal studies with client groups and research of others' experiences produced criteria, guidelines, and formats for each component of this model. I systematically analyzed and used feedback from all participants in these mentoring programs—coordinators, mentors, protégés, and bosses—to refine the model.

What Is Mentoring?

What is this phenomenon called *mentoring*? In the popular comic strip *Doonesbury* (1984), Gary B. Trudeau has the influential person saying, "I didn't even know it was a verb." Misconceptions abound about who a mentor is and what a mentor does. Are all the writers of these articles on mentoring describing the same type of relationship and activities? I think not. The definition of mentoring used in this book is: *a deliberate pairing of a more skilled or experienced person with a lesser skilled or experienced one, with the agreed-upon goal of having the lesser skilled person grow and develop specific competencies.*

Some recent articles on mentoring describe situations in which a person's experiences and behaviors have been positively influenced by another who was what I would call a role model rather than a mentor. The influencer may not even know that he or she is viewed as someone to emulate. The distant star who attracts a number of imitators is not a mentor, by my definition, because only the imitators know of the influence. An influential person may also affect the growth or career of another by acting as a sponsor. For example, when an opportunity for promotion or a plum assignment opens up, the sponsor mentions the name of a favored person. In these cases, the sponsors certainly know what they are doing; however, the beneficiaries may be totally unaware of the support or favors given. In contrast, a mentor and protégé enter into an overt agreement to interact in certain ways to facilitate the learning, growth, and skill development of the protégé.

I make a clear distinction between facilitated mentoring and other forms of structured or formal mentoring. Facilitated mentoring is a structure and series of processes designed to create effective mentoring relationships, guide the desired behavior change of those involved, and evaluate the results for the protégés, the mentors, and the organization. Facilitated mentoring typically includes these components:

- A design that meets the perceived needs of the organization
- Criteria and a process for the selection of protégés
- Strategies and tools ior diagnosing the developmental needs of protégés
- Criteria and a process for qualifying mentors
- Orientation to the responsibilities of the role for both mentors and protégés
- Strategies for matching mentors and protégés on the basis of skills to be developed and compatibility
- A negotiated agreement between mentor, protégé, and boss (if appropriate)
- A coordinator responsible for maintaining the program and supporting the relationships
- Formative evaluation to make necessary adjustments to the program
- Summative evaluation to determine outcomes for the organization, the mentors, and the protégés

Many different kinds of mentoring programs exist in a wide variety of organizations and appear to meet particular needs. For example, in a study of peer relationships Kram and Isabella (1985) found indicators that peers can provide career and psychosocial functions similar to those provided in a hierarchical mentoring alliance. A pairing of peers for mutual support may in effect be mentoring, but I would not call such an arrangement a facilitated mentoring program.

Similarly, a systematic approach to organizational change, sometimes called organizational development, for implementing a mentoring process has been described by others (Beer, 1980; Kram, 1986b). Our experience indicates that merely changing the structure of the organization will not result in a mentoring program. A striking example of the failure of mandating structural change in organizations is found in the performance-appraisal system. Most organizations have a policy that requires managers and supervisors to appraise the performance of subordinates. They assign elaborate forms and mandate a rigid hierarchy of approvals. In practice, however, we hear many people say, "I have not had an appraisal for two or three years!" In organizations that structure mentoring by mandating that supervisors do it and even making it part of performance appraisal, it is highly unlikely that the responsibility is actually carried out. No amount of structure will cause a desired program to work unless there is a systematic means for bringing about the necessary behavior change of those responsible for the results. With facilitated mentoring this behavior change is the responsibility of the coordinators, mentors, protégés, and their managers, who must maintain the improved behaviors with appropriate reinforcement techniques.

As is implied in our definition of mentoring, the primary purpose of facilitated mentoring is to systematically develop the skills and leadership abilities of the less experienced members of an organization. Facilitated mentoring is appropriate when an organization wants to cause this growth and development to happen, and wants to know that it has. Other desired outcomes for facilitating the process may be improved results for the organization, such as increased productivity, increased quality of service, or reduced costs. (The benefits to the organization and how to realize them are described in Chapter Three.)

Purpose of and Audience for the Book

People often ask me, "How did you get interested in facilitated mentoring anyway? What makes you believe in it so strongly? How can I structure a mentoring program and make it work?" This book is my answer to those questions.

It is unfortunate that most of those who are getting satisfactory results with mentoring are not taking the time to write about it. In addition, the continuing discussions and publications (Zey, 1984; Kram, 1985) have generated a lot of heat around the concept of mentoring but have not shed much light on how to design and implement a mentoring process that will produce the desired results for the organization, the mentor, and the protégé. This book fills that gap. It attempts to gather current research and information on successful experiences with mentoring. Its primary purpose is to illustrate various models of facilitated mentoring and to provide specific guidelines for assessing the need for such a program in an organization and for designing and implementing it. The models described in Part Two include all the components of a viable facilitated mentoring program.

The intended audiences for this book are planners, managers, administrators, and human-resource professionals in any type of industrial, government, health care, nonprofit, or educational organization, small or large. It will also be of value to an individual who is or wants to be a mentor or a protégé.

The guidelines in this book will help you determine whether your organization is ready for a facilitated mentoring program. You will find meaningful answers to these questions:

- What is the gap that facilitated mentoring fills?
- What outcomes and benefits can be derived from facilitating the relationships?
- Can mentoring be structured and still flexible?
- Is our organization ready for such a program?
- How big must the organization be?
- Can the results be measured?
- How does mentoring fit with other training efforts?
- Where do you put the mentoring function?
- Who administers the program?
- How do you budget for it?
- How are mentors prepared?
- How are protégés selected?

The guidelines, examples, and checklists will show you

how to tailor a mentoring process for your own organization. If you want to be a mentor or find a mentor, this book will provide helpful information on mentoring relationships and how to make them work.

How This Book Is Designed and Organized

This book is designed to give you quick access to the information you need most. You do not have to read the book from front to back. For example, if you are ready to implement a facilitated mentoring program, you can get on with it by skipping to Chapter Six, where you will find detailed descriptions of each component of a facilitated mentoring model, then to Chapters Seven through Thirteen, where the specifics of mentor and protégé selection, coordinator responsibilities, negotiated agreements, and evaluation are illustrated. Because of this design, readers who do choose to read from cover to cover will find some key information repeated. Scan through the following descriptions and find the chapters that best suit your needs.

The first two chapters trace the evolution of mentoring from early Greek mythology to the present and describe why increasing numbers of organizations are implementing mentoring programs.

Chapter One: What Mentoring Is — What It Is Not

- Gives a brief history of the term *mentor*
- Discusses terminology used in mentoring processes
- Defines what I mean by mentoring in this book

Chapter Two: Mentoring at Work in Organizations

- Relates the experiences of some people who have benefited from a mentoring relationship to illustrate the broad spectrum of mentor/protégé interaction
- Describes trends in the ways mentoring is being used in organizations
- Cites some of the motives for the increasing interest in facilitated mentoring programs

The next three chapters look at what's in it for everybody and what might go wrong. If you have your own list of pros and cons, this section will give you the opportunity to examine the issues closely.

Chapter Three: The Upside and the Downside for the Organization

- Looks at the benefits organizations can gain and the potential problems they face with mentoring programs

Chapter Four: Payoffs and Penalties for the Protégé

- Discusses the positive and negative aspects of the mentoring relationship for the protégé

Chapter Five: The Mentor's Motivation and Concerns

- Explains why a person would willingly take on the role of mentor
- Lists stumbling blocks that mentors and the organization must guard against

In Chapter Six, models and descriptions of programs structured for the public sector, private industry, health care, and educational institutions are presented along with a generic model of a facilitated mentoring program. You may find it helpful to scan these models before reading further in the book to become familiar with the typical components included in facilitated mentoring programs.

Chapter Six: Mentoring Models and Applications

- Illustrates and describes the key elements recommended for a facilitated mentoring program
- Six applications of other facilitated mentoring programs used in the public and private sector are illustrated, with brief annotations of the activities in each component of that mentoring process

Chapters Seven through Twelve provide detailed guide-

lines for designing, implementing, and coordinating a facilitated mentoring program. The material here can be a primary
resource for anyone who may be involved as a program designer,
evaluator, coordinator, mentor, or protégé. You can use the
checklists at the ends of these chapters to gather the data needed
to make important decisions about implementing facilitated
mentoring in your organization.

*Chapter Seven: Assessing Needs and Determining
Organizational Readiness*

- Discusses how to decide whether your organization needs a
  mentoring program and whether the culture of the organization will support such a program

*Chapter Eight: Structuring the Mentor Role: Qualifications,
Recruitment, Selection, and Rewards*

- Gives tips on mentor qualifications and recruitment and on
  making the mentoring role work

*Chapter Nine: Selecting Protégés and Diagnosing
Their Development Needs*

- Outlines strategies for identifying protégé candidates and
  suggests criteria for selecting protégés
- Explains the importance of individual development planning and how to do it

Chapter Ten: Involving the Boss Who Is Not the Mentor

- Lists problems likely to be encountered in the mentor/
  protégé/boss triangle and outlines ways to make the relationship work comfortably

*Chapter Eleven: The Coordinator: Selection,
Training, and Responsibilities*

- Describes the coordinator's responsibilities
- Discusses the types of skills a coordinator needs

Chapter Twelve: Negotiating Sound Mentoring Agreements

- Suggests areas in which parameters must be set in the mentor/protégé agreement
- Explains what to do when the agreement doesn't work

Chapter Thirteen: Evaluating Program Effectiveness

- Describes issues in evaluation
- Gives how-tos for designing evaluations
- Discusses which outcomes should be tracked and how to track them

Chapter Fourteen: Gender, Culture, and Relationship Concerns

- Discusses how differences in sex, race, and age can be beneficial to the mentor/protégé relationship
- Suggests realistic approaches for dealing with relationship problems when they come up
- Discusses several objections that may be expressed by others in the organization: Mentoring is too costly; it causes jealousy; it produces clones

Chapter Fifteen: Making Facilitated Mentoring Work

- Summarizes our recommendations for using facilitated mentoring in organizations

Acknowledgments

The risk of giving well-deserved credit to the many people who contributed to this book is that someone will be missed. Still there are those whose special support must be acknowledged. "With Marna Owen" is a short phrase that speaks volumes to all who know how we work in collaboration. Her creativity, willingness to work hard, and caring have truly made this formidable project doable. She leads a long list of protégés who have persisted in testing every facet of the mentoring relationship, notably Teresa Angwin, Lee Avant, Michelle Jurika, Kelsey Kenfield, Marcy Lambert, Julie Pruitt, Marlys Thompson, and Karen Viano.

I thank all the clients in organizations in which I have worked and learned about the art and craft of improving work performance. Considerable credit goes to those whose careful efforts and feedback have made facilitated mentoring work much better, especially Jim Challis, Linda Crosby DeBerry, Skip Everitt, Rusty Glazer, Rich Laveroni, and Dave Schwandt.

I am especially grateful to Joan Minninger, who helped me over the stumbling blocks; to Howard H. McFann, whose coaching has done so much to clarify for me the value of effective evaluation; and for the great gifts of time and caring criticism given by those who read and gave feedback on the many iterations of the manuscript: Roger Addison, Mike Barber, Marcy Lambert, Marna Owen, Scott Peavler, Russell Robb, and Walt Thurn.

The manuscript itself was enriched and improved by the research and editing done by Marna Owen, Kathe Rickel, and Karen Viano, just as my life has been enriched by their support and friendship.

I would also like to thank the Jossey-Bass editors and staff for their support and encouragement, and Leonard and Zeace Nadler for inviting me to do the book and for their helpful comments.

Oakland, California   Margo Murray
January 1991

The Authors

Margo Murray is president of MMHA The Managers' Mentors, Inc., an international consulting firm established in 1974. She received an A.A. degree (1957) from American River College in business and psychology; a B.S. degree (1963) from California State University, Sacramento, in business administration; and her M.B.A. degree (1977) from John F. Kennedy University in advanced management theory.

Murray's main research and professional contributions have been in organizational needs assessment and in the analysis, design, development, implementation, and evaluation of performance systems. Her innovations include application of a criterion-referenced approach to management skill development, and her models and materials are used by associates in public and private organizations in several countries. Her custom-designed programs and articles have won professional awards and White House recognition for excellence.

She was elected in 1965 to Beta Gamma Sigma, national honor society in business, for her graduate research. In 1979 she was honored as an Outstanding Member of the National Society for Performance and Instruction; in 1984 was awarded its highest honor, Member for Life; and served as president in 1986–87. In 1988 the alumni association of California State University, Sacramento, recognized her "innovative contributions to her profession both nationally and internationally and her creative leadership and dedication to promoting strong mentoring programs" with the Distinguished Service Award.

Murray's management and consulting skills were honed in line and staff positions with Pacific Telephone and in management information systems and as a budget officer with the U.S. Air Force. She serves on the boards of the University of San Francisco School of Business and the International Federation of Training and Development Organizations, and since 1990 on the board of regents of John F. Kennedy University.

Marna A. Owen, senior associate with MMHA The Managers' Mentors, Inc., is a skilled analyst, designer, and project manager. Her B.A. degree (1978) was awarded by the University of Michigan in psychology.

As a writer and editor specializing in educational and training materials, Owen has developed twelve texts for high school students with special needs and has collaborated on the design and development of numerous corporate training programs. Owen's experience as a deputy probation officer provided relevant practice in crisis management, interviewing, and communicating with clients of many ethnic, cultural, and economic backgrounds.

BEYOND THE MYTHS AND MAGIC OF MENTORING

The Mentoring Concept, Benefits, and Pitfalls

Part One begins by tracing the evolution of the mentoring concept as it is described in mythological, religious, popular, and research literature. You may wish to skip the first two chapters if you have already decided to implement a mentoring program and are less interested in the history than in the how-tos.

Chapter One describes the evolution and language of mentoring. It discusses what mentoring is and what it isn't at this stage of the evolutionary process. The roles of those involved in various mentoring processes are described as a framework for understanding the components of a facilitated mentoring model.

To illustrate the many ways in which a mentor and protégé interact, Chapter Two includes descriptions of the experiences of and quotes from a few famous people who have commented on the benefits they received from a mentoring relationship. The examples were selected to dispel the myth that mentoring is a rare, magical happening. Those quoted are employed in the arts, sciences, and industry, yet all credit mentoring for preparing them for their life's work.

It is probably safe to say that every organization has benefited from the contribution of a person who was stimulated by a mentoring relationship. The question Who has had a helpful mentor?, posed to thousands of people in our presentations and workshops on mentoring, has always elicited a positive response from a high percentage of participants. Sparkles come to eyes as the magic of these exceptional relationships comes to mind. Admittedly the sample is biased; however, our literature searches and individual interview data support this conclusion. Popular journals and magazines have reported many examples of informal mentoring that have met with varying degrees of success. Chapter Two relates some of those noteworthy experiences and then describes a number of motives for the increasing interest in structured mentoring programs.

Chapter Two also discusses the movement toward structured mentoring. Survey data from an international study are reported to provide a general overview of the trends toward structured mentoring in hundreds of organizations worldwide. Some managers and administrators believe it is impossible to structure this process, accepting the theory that the relationship is more likely to jell when it happens spontaneously. Nevertheless, more and more organizations are proving the feasibility of facilitating the mentoring process in systematic ways with good results. (Several of those organizations have generously contributed examples from their own programs for Chapter Six.) The structure of a mentoring program and the extent to which the mentoring processes are formalized depend on:

- The needs of the organization
- The philosophy of human-resource development within that organization
- The availability of other developmental resources

The viewpoints of the organization, the protégé, and the mentor toward the mentoring relationship are described in Chapters Three, Four, and Five. These chapters provide examples of issues and benefits to each of these participants. As you consider using mentors in your development programs, you will no doubt think of many obstacles you may face in implementation. As one of these "Yes, but. . ." thoughts pops into your mind, jot it down in the margin. Chapters Seven through Twelve will give you many preventive strategies for overcoming these obstacles.

Part One of this book serves two purposes: to review the value of healthy mentoring relationships and to give you some language to use and examples to cite in explaining mentoring to others. If you are already sold on the concept of mentoring and confident of your ability to describe it to others, you may wish to skip to Part Two and get on with preparing to design or audit your own program.

1

What Mentoring Is —
What It Is Not

Before reviewing the beginnings of mentoring, I find it useful to look at the two basic schools of thought about mentoring that exist in today's business world. One is the belief that mentoring can be structured or facilitated; the other is the belief that it can only "happen."

In my definition, *facilitated* mentoring is *a structure and series of processes designed to create effective mentoring relationships, guide the desired behavior change of those involved, and evaluate the results for the protégés, the mentors, and the organization* with the primary purpose of systematically developing the skills and leadership abilities of the less-experienced members of an organization. To clarify the relationship of mentoring to other modes of training and development it may be helpful to define other terms I may use. I define *learning* as an observable change in behavior, and I define *training* as the process of helping someone to learn. Training can occur through the use of self-study texts or interactive videodisk modules, or through modeling, tutoring, and coaching by a mentor or trainer.

Our experience suggests that a process, such as a mentoring program, for helping someone to learn cannot be mandated or made to work solely by structural change. It is essential to get behavior change in the decision makers and participants in order to realize the potential benefits. Mentoring can create conditions for motivating such changes in behaviors (Murray-

Hicks and Nugent, 1971). In addition, this type of mentoring has a great advantage: By structuring and facilitating the mentoring process, we can prevent the problems that are likely to occur with mismatches. Problems occur in the best of relationships, and a facilitator can assist with solving the problems while protecting the beneficial relationship. Finally, organizations can gather data to track results, measure outcomes, and assess the cost effectiveness of a facilitated mentoring program.

Representatives of the second school of thought, who suggest that true mentoring is spontaneous or informal, caution that it cannot be structured or formalized. In their opinion a structured mentoring relationship lacks a critical, magical ingredient. They see it as an arranged marriage — utilitarian but often lacking passion. Fury (1980) writes that the mentor/protégé relationship is a "mysterious, chemical attraction of two people . . . prompt[ing] them to take the risks inherent in any intensely close relationship" (p. 47). Even some of those researchers who have attempted objective studies of mentoring relationships tend to paint a dismal picture of the prospects of guiding the process. In the report of a two-year study, Premac Associates (1984, p. 55) concluded, "Mentoring . . . seems to work best when it is simply 'allowed to happen.'"

The increasing number of participants in what others call formal programs are evidence against that opinion. To emphasize the importance of maintaining the magic of the pairing while avoiding the stifling effect of excessive structure, I have chosen to use the term *facilitated*: The organization facilitates the beneficial results for mentor, protégé, and the organization itself. When describing my research and experience, I will use the term *facilitated*. When relating the experience of others, I will use their terms — *formal, structured, informal* — with clarifying notations where necessary. More on the language of mentoring and the terms used in this book later in this chapter; for now let's go back to the genesis of the concept.

Evolution of Mentoring

History gives many examples of the value of mentoring. Perhaps the most famous instance was chronicled by Homer in the *Odyssey*. Homer tells us that around 1200 B.C., the adventurer

Odysseus made ready to leave for the siege of Troy. Before sailing, he appointed a guardian to his household. For the next ten years, this guardian acted faithfully as teacher, adviser, friend, and surrogate father to Telemachus, son of Odysseus. The mythical guardian's name was Mentor.

Homer's story reflects one of the oldest attempts by a society to facilitate mentoring. It was customary in ancient Greece for young male citizens to be paired with older males in the hope that each boy would learn and emulate the values of his mentor, usually a friend of the boy's father or a relative.

The Greeks based these relationships on a basic principle of human survival: Humans learn skills, culture, and values directly from other humans whom they look up to or admire. How much of your current behavior stems from interactions with your parents or parental figures? Have you ever stopped in mid-sentence and thought with mock horror, "I sound just like my parents!" This is evidence of how powerful modeling is and can be. Children learn to avoid physical harm through parental warnings and example. They learn to communicate and interact primarily in the family unit. When the interactions are healthy and successful, valuable behavior is copied and repeated. And, unfortunately, unpleasant or destructive behavior is just as likely to be repeated. Humans tend to emulate the behavior they see in others, especially when that behavior is rewarded (Bandura, 1986). Successive generations of family members carry on many of the behaviors and rituals modeled by parents and parental figures.

These same principles of modeling and mentoring have been key elements in the continuity of art, craft, and commerce from ancient times. A good example can be found in the craft guilds that began in the Middle Ages. These societies helped structure the professions of merchant, lawyer, goldsmith, and more. Young boys were traditionally apprenticed to a master, a person who was considered excellent in his trade and who owned a shop or business. The boy lived with the master, worked his way up to journeyman, and finally became a master himself by taking an examination or producing an exemplary work in his profession (hence the word *masterpiece*). Often the new master would take over the business at the old master's retirement or death. It was also traditional for him to marry the master's widow and take over the family responsibilities. Through this form of structured mentoring, the craft guilds controlled the quality of work and the wages of their professions and passed on valuable social and political connections.

The master/apprentice relationship was eventually transformed into the employer/employee relationship by industrial society. Employers' focus shifted away from maintaining quality and tradition toward increasing their profits. What benefited the master no longer benefited the apprentice. Lower wages and longer work hours eventually gave birth to the unions. The turbulent era of worker against management was born.

Informal mentoring has its place in history as well. Academic research, popular literature, and personal accounts tout the value of informal mentoring in every conceivable vocation and avocation. Using historical records, and acknowledging that the classification was sometimes based on conjectures, writers have looked at mentor/protégé pairs ranging from Sir Thomas More, English statesman and author of *Utopia*, and Thomas Linacre and William Grocyn in the 1490s, to Michael Jackson and Diana Ross in the 1970s (Head and Gray, 1988).

Protégés describe the magical richness of these developmental exchanges in glowing generalities. Mary Cassatt reported (McMullen, 1984, p. 293) what it meant to her when the Impressionist artist Edgar Degas took a personal interest in her professional career and became her mentor: "I accepted with joy. Now I could work with absolute independence without considering the opinion of a jury. I had already recognized who were my true masters. I admired Manet, Courbet, and Degas. I took leave of conventional art. I began to live."

In such historical informal relationships, the mentor may have assisted in career advancement or guided the protégé through the political pathways of a profession or an organization. Less frequently, the contact may have included coaching the protégé in the development of specific skills. No matter how minimal or extensive, this individual attention almost always had positive results for the protégé, such as increased professional recognition or job effectiveness. For the mentor, a sense of accomplishment came from having made a contribution to the growth of another person.

Since the mid-1970s great attention has been paid to both informal and facilitated mentoring relationships and their impact in the business world. As companies grow larger and more impersonal, their need for person-to-person mentoring grows. In fact, mentoring has been described as "an American management innovation" (Odiorne, 1985, p. 63). For a company to survive and thrive, it must have a mechanism for regenerating itself from within. "That simple fact epitomizes what is now a Jewel [Tea] tradition. . . . These mentor relationships develop leaders" (Collins and Scott, 1978, p. 207).

The movement of women into the upper ranks of management also created a renewed interest in mentoring. Kathleen Fury, editor-in-chief of *Your Place* magazine (1980, p. 43) called "mentor mania" one of the "first managerial fascinations whose popular origins can be traced to a concern with women's careers rather than men's."

However, mentoring is no longer associated only with women and minorities. The competitiveness of the global economy is reuniting the values of worker and manager; both are beginning to recognize the need for leadership and quality. Many organizations support the mentoring process and provide structures and procedures for carrying it out — facilitated mentoring — for all employees who seek new skills and knowledge. At Sony (Akio Morita, interview with author, 1988), for example, all new employees wear a small green circle on their identification badges. The green circle tells experienced employees to stop and give their full attention to the new employee, to share know-how and the ways of the corporate culture. Akio Morita, the chairman of the board of Sony Corporation, has a clear vision of the role this philosophy plays in Sony's success (1988): "We are making ourselves responsible for their education and well-being. I consider it my job as a manager to do everything I can to nurture the curiosity of people I work with" (p. 2).

Does the ancient concept of mentoring have its place in today's modern business world? In the technological twentieth century, the need for facilitated mentoring is greater than ever. Organizations are still made up of people—people who require ever greater skills for mastering the increasingly complex issues and tasks in every working environment. The complexity of today's organizations, coupled with an increasing emphasis on cost containment, makes facilitated mentoring an attractive, low-cost strategy for developing a skilled work force.

It is true that the chemistry of many informal mentoring experiences cannot be automatically created through structure. But facilitated mentoring can give a protégé the same opportunity offered the apprentice of medieval times—a chance to learn from a master. Good and not so good mentoring experiences can be used to design strategies for encouraging the richness and magic in a relationship. Magic and chemistry? Well, most magicians have a skillful assistant, and the most productive chemical research has always been carried on in carefully controlled environments. Assisting, guiding, and controlling the mentoring process have proven to be feasible in both historical and modern times. Is it worth the effort? Using the data and guidelines in this book, you will be able to answer that question for your organization and for yourself.

Language of Mentoring

Although Hennig and Jardim advised ambitious women to "look for a coach, a godfather or godmother, a mentor, and advocate" (1977, p. 162), few organizations used the word *mentor* in facilitated programs until recently. More common were the terms offered by Levinson (1986): coach, adviser, senior adviser, counselor, and experience leader. The mentor is also at times designated as the master, guide, exemplar, luminary, trainer, instructor, leader, and boss.

What's in a name? The titles given to the various roles in a mentoring program can reflect the organization's philosophy, style, and culture. The culture of an organization determines the titles that are most acceptable for each of the roles, particularly that of mentor. (Culture is defined here as the shared beliefs and biases that shape the way people are treated in an organization.) We can use the word *coach* to demonstrate the link between company culture and mentoring terminology. *Coach* has become popular in companies concerned with productivity and competition. The spreading interest in what is called the Japanese style of management has focused managers on team efforts rather than on individual achievement. The popularity of the role of the coach is a natural outcome of that team emphasis.

Because a facilitated mentoring program can be a major investment for an organization of any size, it is unwise to jeopardize the full realization of benefits by choosing an objectionable title for the key players in the program. The following discussion clarifies various titles and describes how they are used in this book. The terms used for the roles performed by those involved in mentoring programs are many and varied (Fagan and Walter, 1982; Kram, 1985; Levinson, 1986). These terms will be used in this book as they are used by the organizations providing examples, and, where appropriate, they will be differentiated from the terms used to describe facilitated mentoring in the how-to parts of this book.

Definitions: Who Is and Isn't a Mentor?

Role model, sponsor, and mentor—how are they alike and how do they differ? A careful look at each of these roles will provide the answer.

Sponsor. A *sponsor* can be an active booster or advocate for any number of people, all at the same time. For example, a sponsor can finance the company baseball team, recommend several candidates for promotional opportunities, or establish scholarship funds at the local university. A sponsor is constrained only by time and generosity. On the receiving end, a fortunate individual may have several sponsors. The sponsoring relationship is informal, with neither person making any commitments of responsibility or interaction. The sponsor most certainly knows who is being sponsored; however, the sponsored person may or may not know who the sponsor is. The sponsor role can continue indefinitely, as long as the sponsor sees a need and is willing and able to continue in the role.

Activities of a sponsor of another individual in the business world include:

- Making introductions to top people in the organization
- Making introductions to others with influence in the industry or profession
- Making recommendations for advancement
- Reflecting power on the sponsored person by publicly praising accomplishments and abilities
- Facilitating entry into meetings and activities usually attended by high-level people
- Serving as a confidant
- Offering guidance in the customs of the organization

Role models. Role models can perform the same activities as a sponsor or can simply be held in high regard by any number of people without even knowing that they are viewed in this favorable light. Undoubtedly someone like Malcolm Forbes was a role model to hundreds of aspiring business students, whether they'd met him or not. Similarly, an individual may have several role models at one time. There is no particular structure to the role-modeling relationship. It can continue as long as the observer sees positive behaviors to emulate.

Role models often exhibit:

- Success
- Exemplary behavior in achievement and style
- An ability to get things done
- Knowledge of organization policy and philosophy
- Apparent enjoyment of position and accomplishment

Mentor. By contrast, in a facilitated mentoring process there is typically one *mentor* to one protégé, and each knows what is expected of the other. The mentor carries out some or even all of the functions of the sponsor and role model in a relationship structured around the skills that the protégé wants to develop.

In addition, a mentor may agree to perform one or more of the following functions:

- Act as a source of information on the mission and goals of the organization
- Provide insight into the organization's philosophy of human-resource development
- Tutor specific skills, effective behavior, and how to function in the organization
- Give feedback on observed performances
- Coach activities that will add to experience and skill development
- Serve as a confidant in times of personal crises and problems
- Assist the protégé in plotting a career path
- Meet with the protégé at agreed time intervals for feedback and planning
- Agree to a *no-fault* conclusion of the mentoring relationship when (for any reason) the time is right
- Maintain the integrity of the relationship between the protégé and the natural boss

Such activities are clearly different from the more casual interactions that occur spontaneously with role models and sponsors. Strategies for avoiding duplication of effort or potential conflict with the line supervisor are discussed in the relevant chapters of Part Two.

Protégé. Popular labels for the *protégé* include mentee, candidate, apprentice, aspirant, advisee, counselee, trainee, and student. Less popular synonyms are follower, subordinate, applicant, hopeful, and seeker. In a facilitated program, the candidate for protégé will have, at a minimum, these characteristics:

- Willingness to assume responsibility for his or her own growth and development

- Assessed potential to succeed at one or more levels above the present position in the organization
- Ability to perform in more than one skill area
- A record of seeking challenging assignments and new responsibilities
- Receptivity to feedback and coaching

From here on in this book, the words *mentor* and *protégé* imply these characteristics and responsibilities unless otherwise noted. Part Two gives additional insight into the factors that influence the choice of titles for mentors and protégés in organizations.

This brief discussion has provided a historical overview of mentoring and working definitions of the mentor and protégé roles. Chapter Two takes a closer look at the reasons for the increasing interest in facilitated mentoring in public and private organizations.

2

Mentoring at Work in Organizations

A list of those who publicly acknowledge the value of their mentoring relationships resembles a Who's Who of the professions, business, sports, arts, and social activism. The following comments on the interaction of these selected notable pairs illustrate the deep and continuing impact of mentoring relationships in many environments. Some of these pairings obviously just happened. Other connections were apparently initiated through work or professional proximity. A few of the relationships were planned and deliberate. Interestingly enough, even when the mentor and protégé worked in the same field, their work styles were often quite different. The specific quotes were selected to illustrate the wide variety of benefits to one or both parties in a mentoring relationship.

Selected Examples of Mentoring Benefits

Acting. Larry D. Clark, dean of arts and sciences, University of Missouri, Columbia, was a mentor to Tom Berenger, Academy Award–Nominee actor. Berenger, who came to the University of Missouri as a journalism major, tried out for a play that Clark was directing. The relationship sparked, and Berenger changed his major to theater. Clark (interview by author, 1990) says, "Tom soaked up technique so fast that it never seemed as if it was a mentor/protégé relationship. It was more like a mutual learning situation—all of us used his talent to refine our work. He made me realize fully how much the mentor can learn from the exceptional protégé." From the viewpoint of the protégé, Berenger (interview by author, 1990) comments, "In the theater, you often learn without knowing where or how it happened. A good mentor helps you to know when you've got it right and, more importantly, helps you know how to do it again. I believe that holds true for all walks of life."

Art. Nelli Bar, mentor to Richard Hunt, sculptor, saw the opportunity to shape the budding career of a fifteen-year-old in a sculpture class at The Junior School of the Art Institute of Chicago (Reeve, 1985, p. 13). After a thirty-year relationship, Hunt recalls, "One of the most important things that an artist has to decide is whether to take the notion of a career in art seriously. Her counsel was crucial at the time I was making that decision."

Gas Company. "There's absolutely no doubt that if it hadn't been for Ruth Royston, my life would have been entirely different," Richard C. Vierbuchen, executive vice-president of Washington Gas Light Company, says of his mentor (Hogan, 1984, p. 47). "I probably never would have gone to college if it hadn't been for her."

Finance. Vice-President of Public Relations John Charnay was attracted to Glendale Federal Savings and Loan because of the philosophy of individual responsibility for career development (Hogan, 1984, p. 28). "The Chairman of the Board . . . was once the public relations director here, and that's why I joined the company in the first place; I wanted that kind of [mentoring] relationship."

Law. Leo Herzel, partner and cochairman of Mayer Brown & Platt, was mentor to Susan Getzendanner, U.S. district court judge, who says (Reeve, 1985, p. 9): "We have very few common interests apart from the law. . . . We have totally different backgrounds: I'm Irish-Catholic; he's Jewish. He's very intellectual, very cultured; I'm more people-oriented. Yet, in the entire twelve years . . . there were only three or four times when we misunderstood each other. He was never threatened by my success."

Major League Baseball. James Kittle was mentor to his son, White Sox outfielder Ron Kittle (Reeve, 1985, p. 9). "He's taught me most of what I know," says Ron. "He never pushed me into anything; he helped me out."

Politics. Paul Douglas, former U.S. senator, was mentor to Paul Simon, U.S. senator (Reeve, 1985, p. 12). "He was a great inspiration to me, . . . a guy of real integrity. . . . In his auto-biography, Paul [Douglas] listed me as one of the reasons he had faith in the future."

Power Utility. Tom Ayers, past chairman of the board and president of Commonwealth Edison, was mentor to Jim O'Con-nor, who now holds that position (Reeve, 1985, p. 8). "I learned from Tom that people are more important than methods or machines. He's also taught me the value of loyalty."

Religion. Joseph Cardinal Bernardin, archbishop of Chi-cago, was a protégé of the late Paul J. Hallinan, archbishop of Atlanta, and John Cardinal Dearden, former archbishop of Detroit (Reeve, 1985, p. 12). "What used to frighten me was that he [Archbishop Hallinan] had much more confidence in me than I had in myself."

Scientific Medicine. Leon Jacobson, professor emeritus at the Pritzker School of Medicine, was mentor to Janet Rowley, Blum-Riese Distinguished Service Professor of Medicine at Pritzker (Reeve, 1985, p. 11). "He took a real chance with me, with no likelihood that his gamble would pay off. I had no credentials as a scientist then."

Social Activists. Dr. Benjamin E. Mays was mentor to Mar-tin Luther King, Jr. ("Obituary of Dr. Benjamin Mays," 1984, p. B2). King was heard to say that he was "awakened both intellectually and spiritually by my mentor, Dr. Benjamin E. Mays."

Symphony. Principal French horn of the Chicago Symphony Orchestra, Dale Clevenger, was a protégé of Arnold Jacobs and Adolf Herseth of the Chicago Symphony Orchestra (Reeve, 1985, p. 13). "He [Arnold Jacobs] taught me, in case of an error, to try again and do better. I frankly doubt that I'd be where I am today if it weren't for him."

Technology. Tom Watson, Sr., founder of IBM, learned his craft under John Patterson at National Cash Register (Odiorne, 1985, p. 66). "Look at the list of today's senior executives of major American corporations and you will find an astonishing record of their having 'descended' from just a few leaders, and that each one worked for a great mentor."

The list could go on. Many people proclaim the positive influence of mentors on their lives—particularly people in business and increasingly those in nonprofit organizations. An international management-consulting firm, Heidrick and Struggles, surveyed 1,250 prominent men and women executives in the late 1970s (Roche, 1979, p. 15) to determine the factors contributing to their success. Nearly two-thirds of those surveyed reported having had a mentor or sponsor. The positive results were both measurable and had less tangible indicators. "Executives who have had a mentor earned more money at a younger age, . . . are happier with their progress and derive greater pleasure from their work."

It is highly likely that most of those mentoring relationships just happened through some spontaneous interaction of the two people. Either party may have initiated the contract. The protégé may have thought, "I'd like to learn more from that person," or may have seen that person do something that had good results; success is seductive. Or the mentor may have been unconsciously attracted to the fresh perspective of the protégé and may have offered a few suggestions for furthering the protégé's work. No matter who initiated the first exchange, both parties undoubtedly felt good about the results of that interaction and sought additional contact. The seeds of a productive relationship were sown in fertile ground while shared achievement continued to strengthen the bond.

Many of the relationships that have been described in popular publications have been such happenstance occurrences. A sales manager in a furniture-manufacturing firm (Blotnick, 1984, p. 9) expressed it this way: "I'm looking, but I'm keeping a low profile; if you're too open about it your search might backfire. It seems to me that searching for a mentor is a lot like looking for love: It has to sneak up on you if it's really going to be right." However, Blotnick's survey of twenty-five executives concluded that without some guidance there is "nothing surefire about. . . finding a suitable mentor" (p. 9). Articles (Robinson, 1990; Zuckerman, 1990) now indicate that the trend is toward putting some formal structure into the mentoring process.

Motives for Facilitated Mentoring

What perceived needs are generating this increased interest in formalized mentoring? According to Zey (1986), five major social and economic trends are creating problems for the modern corporation: the quest for innovation, the merger explosion, the changing composition of the work force, the coming labor shortage, and the emergence of the cross-cultural corporation. Zey suggests that mentoring can help solve the problems created by these trends. These and several additional phenomena may be motivating executives and administrators in a variety of organizations to consider increasing the amount of structure in their mentoring processes.

Need for Leadership. The research of Bennis and Nanus (1985, p. 188) indicates the trend can be attributed partly to the search for leaders. "Nearly all leaders are highly proficient in learning from experience. Most were able to identify a small number of mentors and key experiences that powerfully shaped their philosophies, personalities, aspirations, and operating styles."

Irrelevance of Theory-Based Formal Education to Real-World Management and Administrative Needs. A study of the curricula of five business schools (Murray-Hicks, 1977) revealed that the offered courses addressed only half of the sixteen skills identified as vital signs for mastery in management. Skills relevant to organizing and planning, quality of decisions, leadership, behavior flexibility, inner work standards, group process, technical job knowledge, and salesmanship/marketing were taught in one or more courses at each university. But none of the business schools offered courses with the stated objectives of developing students' skills in decisiveness, creativity, written communication, oral communication, tolerance of uncertainty, resistance to stress, energy, or use of personal power. The results of the study confirmed the hypothesis that a significant gap exists between the skills required for successful management performance and the skills taught in a traditional business school. It would be naive to suggest that any one business school curriculum will ever fulfill all needs for all students, although certainly the relevance of courses taught in most schools could be improved. However, four of the skills that are most often neglected in school curricula—decisiveness, tolerance of uncertainty, resistance to stress, and use of personal power—are particularly appropriate for modeling and coaching by a skillful mentor.

Dissatisfaction with the Functional Illiteracy of Entry-Level Employees. Graduates from secondary schools are entering the work force unprepared to perform at a satisfactory level. Basic career and life skills such as reading and simple mathematics are inadequate. The U.S. Department of Education estimates that the functionally illiterate now account for 30 percent of unskilled, 29 percent of semiskilled, and 11 percent of managerial, professional, and technical employees (Zemke, 1989). Companies are recognizing the long-term impact on their businesses of these skill deficiencies. CBS News reported in July 1989 that BellSouth, with a long-standing reputation for hiring people into entry-level jobs and promoting to supervisory, management, and executive levels from within, made a sizable contribution to special programs for improving basic skills training in secondary schools in their employment area. Even with such special programs, the deficiencies will not be eliminated overnight. Peer-group mentors in entry-level positions may be an effective resource to fill part of the gap.

Disenchantment with Traditional Training Programs. There is a growing disenchantment with conventional educational and training programs offered within organizations. Most organizations offer a menu of generic management and supervisory training programs—for example, courses in time management and basic communication—as well as technical or job-specific courses. Such skills training is essential, and we are not suggesting that it be replaced by mentoring. However, when training courses use traditional academic formats such as lecture and presentation, the busy manager gets frustrated and bored. Often the content of courses aimed at the "average" person is an insult to experienced professionals. Many times there is no follow-up to determine whether skills are applied back on the job. All too often bosses lack the motivation or ability to reinforce and build on skills learned by trainees in a course.

The fad of new-age training has also met serious opposition in the business world and in government. When many employees expressed skepticism and outright fear of such programs such as Charles Krone's Leadership Development Seminars, Werner Erhard's est (once known as Erhard Seminars Training, later as Erhard's Transformational Technologies), and other value- and culture-change processes, a number of organizations stopped such external training. Pender, in an investigative series for the *San Francisco Chronicle* (1987a–f), reported cancellation of such courses by Crown Zellerbach, Tektronix, and others. One of Pender's articles in this series was titled "PacBell Stops 'Kroning.'" Peter Waldman, staff reporter for the *Wall Street Journal*, described the mixed reactions of, rifts among, and dissent of employees coerced into learning "New Agespeak" (1987). Constance Horner, director of the U.S. Office of Personnel Management, discovered that the government was conducting an exotic management-training course that included subliminal messages intended to promote a sense of well-being.

Horner canceled the course (Havemann, 1987) with increased conviction that management training in the federal government needs improvement.

The bottom line is that attitudinal and behavioral changes are extremely difficult to accomplish, especially for the individual left on his or her own. "While a variety of issues surround motivation to transfer learning to the job, the ones we have found to be important for development and personal change include the perceived organizational support for the training, the individual's willingness to participate in that training, and the personal and professional events occurring in close proximity to the training" (Van Velsor, 1984, p. 1).

Expanding Awareness of Performance Technology. As organizations are downsized, companies are seeking opportunities to increase the cost effectiveness of human-resource development. Fortunately, at the same time they are becoming aware of the efficacy of performance technology. The strategies of performance technology can be applied to the analysis and design of a facilitated mentoring program that is targeted to fill the gap between the skill requirements for a function and its tasks, and the current skills of the job incumbent. Performance technology also provides the strategies for evaluating the impact of the mentoring experience on the competence of the protégé and the results of the organization.

Need to Meet Affirmative-Action Goals. Milestones on affirmative action timetables set for ten or twenty years in the future may originally have been viewed as feasible using ordinary training and development programs. As the deadlines approach and the goals have not been met, the search begins for viable and targeted programs such as mentoring. Currently there is a surge of interest in mentoring programs for women and minorities. Recent queries about our mentoring experiences have come from a broad spectrum of companies and organizations—aerospace, education, telecommunications, glass manufacturing, tobacco, grocery distribution, retail clothing, and accounting—all citing the need to develop women and minorities for management positions to meet affirmative-action goals.

Awareness of the Needs of an Increasingly Diverse Work Force. Employees must pursue professional development and take personal responsibility for their own growth if they wish to maintain required skills. Because few people have the skills and objectivity to assess accurately their own developmental needs, employers must provide the environment and some of the resources that support this growth. The work force of the year 2000 will be an entirely new one, as restructuring efforts provide incentives for early retirement and the new employees are increasingly women and minorities. (A 1988 study done by AT&T [Montana, 1988] projected that 82 percent of new hires will be women, minorities, and immigrants.) Many of those newly hired will have even less ability than current employees to accurately assess their skills relevant to job requirements, particularly beyond entry-level positions. "Employees will come from populations which speak English as a second language, have lower levels of educational attainment and are not very familiar with Western culture. It is time to rethink the role of private corporations as long-term partners in the support of education" (Andrew and Winchell, 1988, p. 91).

A visual scan of any office or shop will illustrate that diversity in the work force is no longer a white and black issue. Supervisors in multicultural work environments find significant differences in workers who are American-born minorities and recent immigrants from those same ethnic groups. Generalizations about groups create trouble, especially in the design of performance-improvement programs. All Asians do not respond to the same structure any more than all Americans do. For example, the strong team concept prevalent among Japanese workers is not shared by workers from Taiwan, where competitiveness is often the norm. Sensitivity to the differences of people within traditional cultural classifications and attention to individual needs and wants will be increasingly important.

Need to Replace an Aging Work Force. The Federal government will face a crisis of competence when 57,000 baby boomers
hit the optional retirement age of fifty-five in the year 2002
(Carmichael, 1988). Most hiring in the public sector takes place
at the clerical and administrative levels, and higher-level positions are filled by promotions from within. Procedures for
moving up from entry levels to middle levels of administration
have long been established. The mounting number of retire-
ments will create a critical need for seasoned executives.

Two agencies, the General Accounting Office (GAO) and
the Internal Revenue Service, are addressing this need by using a
mentoring process to make the younger administrator ready for
executive responsibility. From 1984 to 1989 fifty-five candidates
for the Senior Executive Service in the GAO participated in the
Executive Candidate Development Program (ECDP), which has
a mentoring element (R. R. Glazer, interview by author, 1989).
The ECDP is one component of the overall management-
development plan. Individuals accepted into the ECDP are expected to develop the managerial competence required of leaders at the executive level within eighteen months.

Recognition of Increasing Labor/Management Cooperation.
Training and development programs offered by unions are becoming increasingly comprehensive and sophisticated. Appren-
ticeship is a respected tradition in many crafts and industries. It
is a logical progression from an apprentice/master relationship
to a mentoring relationship designed to produce competence
in high-technology jobs and in areas that are often described as
softer.

Labor and management are beginning to recognize that
to prosper in a changing, increasingly competitive environment
they must change the way they relate to one another. When I was
a line manager in the 1960s and 1970s the unions objected to
managers singling out any of their members for special training
and resisted development plans designed for individuals, such
as a mentoring relationship. Now there is a growing apprecia-
tion among labor and management professionals that cooper-
ative labor systems are more productive than adversarial ones.

"Labor and management must be equipped with *partnership skills* so they can work together to develop a work environment that will meet the challenges of the year 2000 and beyond" (Dinnocenzo, 1988, p. 71).

Recognition of the Changes Caused by Restructuring Companies and the Economy. Restructuring companies need strong, generalist managers who can make a successful transition from one industry or technical area to another. Also needed are managers who can move from a professional or technical specialty, such as engineering, to a totally different function, such as marketing manager. This need will grow as jobs in the service sector increase while jobs in the production sector decrease. "The American work force has shifted from manufacturing goods to delivering services" (Harriman, 1985, p. 16).

Churn and change in functions within organizations will cause people to change career fields many times. The analysts speculate that more than one million poorly equipped applicants will need to be trained each year between 1990 and 2000. Once trained, however, they are not likely to remain qualified, as most organizations are expected to restructure multiple times. Most employees will have three or more entirely different career experiences. Older, more experienced workers not only will have to learn new skills but also will have to learn those skills from younger supervisors, mentors, or peers.

Need for Succession Planning and Management Development. With the fast growth of service and knowledge organizations, society is becoming increasingly dependent on what Sveiby and Lloyd call knowhow (1987, p. 18). "Knowhow companies solve complex, nonstandardized problems, traditional service companies solve simple ones." Example of traditional service companies are banks, fast-food restaurants, and machinery repair shops. Knowhow companies are those that provide services totally adapted to the client such as law firms, portfolio managers, and telecommunications-design companies.

Succession planning becomes increasingly important in service and knowledge-based organizations. The most skilled professional or technical person may be the poorest candidate for manager. The skills required to troubleshoot an equipment malfunction or sell a product are quite different from the skills necessary for managing a group of professional engineers or salespeople. The technical person's desire to "do it better than those guys can" gets in the way of managing and leading the effort. However, selection of top management from outside an organization still is the exception rather than the rule. Most top people grow and develop in an up-through-the-ranks process. Therefore, implementation of a succession planning program is critical. "If it is to survive long-term, the professional organization must develop enough competent 'seniors' to discharge the responsibilities of top management" (Sveiby and Lloyd, 1987, p. 110).

Movement Toward Structured Mentoring

Whatever the stimulus, the interest in structured mentoring is growing. In the United States, organizations that have some type of structured mentoring program can be found in industry, education, and government. A partial list of those mentioned in various publications includes American College, AT&T, Bell Labs, California Women in Government, Federal Express, the GAO, General Motors, Glendale Federal Savings, Hughes Aircraft, J.C. Penney, Jewel Tea, Merrill Lynch, and New York University.

This increasing interest in structured mentoring is not limited to the United States. One international survey (PA Personnel Services, 1986) conducted in the 1980s in eight countries found sixty-seven organizations (18 percent of those surveyed) with formal (their term) mentoring programs. The majority of organizations that had implemented these programs reported that they were pleased with the results of the mentoring efforts. Only one said the program was unsuccessful. Sixty-four percent of the organizations with formal programs characterized the programs as totally or largely successful, and 93 percent planned to continue these programs. Seventy-five percent of the individuals who commented on the programs viewed them as successful. The organizations perceived the main benefit of a formal mentoring program to be improved succession planning and management development. In this survey almost half the "schemes" (their term) had been in operation for only one to two years. An additional eighty-eight of the reporting organizations were considering instituting formal mentoring programs in the near future.

Setting up a mentoring program specifically designed to benefit the organization is a relatively new trend. Development for future career positions has been largely limited to top executives and often given as a reward rather than because of an assessed need. Typically, the training for other employees has been directed at current job skills. Now mentoring programs are being instituted with the explicit goal of increasing company profitability by making individuals more productive. Other companies—feeling the direct financial impact of being fined for not complying with affirmative-action agreements—are investigating ways to establish mentoring programs specifically for women and minorities.

However, Levine (1985) concluded from a survey of corporate development programs that formal mentorships probably constitute only 3 to 4 percent of the mentoring that is actually occurring. Structuring the mentoring processes may be uncommon because there is a lack of data on just how cost-effective it is. Many organizations that have implemented mentoring programs do not have ways to measure the program's direct impact on productivity or individual performance. Hence, other organizations do not have the hard figures to convince them to try mentoring. One might think that the need for evaluating such programs is obvious. If there is a costly gap in capability that needs to be filled, astute managers will want to know the cost of the solution and whether that solution really works. However, costly programs of all sorts have been put in place because a manager or administrator wanted that program, not because of an assessed need. Rarely is the evaluation and tracking mechanism designed into the program itself. More often an evaluation is done only when someone questions the costs. Strategies for evaluating a facilitated mentoring process are suggested in Chapter Thirteen.

Also, deliberately pairing mentors with protégés in a facilitated program may not be acceptable in some organizational cultures. For example, having an employee mentored by someone other than his or her line boss might be seen as disloyal or subversive behavior. This is not to suggest that any culture is right or wrong. Criticism of a culture as being wrong may stimulate a strong defense of the status quo. It will then be even more difficult to bring about the desired changes. An organization's culture evolves over the years and may continue for decades even though the people who helped to shape it are no longer there. Cultural change is a slow process in most environments, and structuring a mentoring program as the sole agent of such change is likely to fail.

Structured or facilitated mentoring is thus not for everyone, and it is also not the magic bullet for solving all organizational ills. Some organizations look to mentoring as a way to avoid the formidable task of developing unskilled managers and supervisors. This solution is shortsighted at best and can create monstrous problems because one then has to work around the managers who lack basic people skills. A mentoring program should be one component of a comprehensive system of people development. For sustained effectiveness, it must be carefully integrated with the other components of that system: training programs, performance appraisals, recruitment. When all managers and supervisors have the skills and strengths to assist their subordinates with career planning, skill development, and growth, the need for a special mentoring program may diminish. However, even then mentors can continue to provide added value by helping prepare people for different functional responsibilities.

Do these current trends, examples, and motives make you think that facilitated mentoring may be worth a try in your organization? Chapters Three, Four, and Five illustrate the benefits and issues of a mentoring process for the organization, the protégé, and the mentor. Chapter Seven presents strategies to help you assess your organization's readiness for a facilitated mentoring program. The specific guidelines given there will help you design your program to realize the full benefits of the mentoring process and avoid many problems.

3

The Upside and the Downside for the Organization

Corporate Executive Fellows (CEF) is an ambitious program whose goal is to develop and provide top-level minority leadership for U.S. corporations. Fellows (protégés) in the program stand to benefit a great deal. Those who pass CEF's tough screening process are offered full tuition in MBA programs at Columbia or Stanford, a $16,000 stipend, and $6,000 worth of computer equipment and software from Hewlett-Packard. Each Fellow must meet the stringent academic standards of the chosen university and complete an eight-month, executive-oriented mentored internship with a corporation such as Citicorp Securities Markets and Investment Bank, Eastman Kodak, or the Equitable Financial Company.

According to George A. Peña, director of the New York City–based CEF program (interview by author, 1990), there are great benefits to the corporations who offer mentoring internships to the CEF fellows. "The corporations are very impressed with the candidates in our program. The candidates are hardworking people and truly courageous to even be in this program. Most companies are looking for qualified, good minority talent. That is our reason for existence. We can guarantee through the design of our program the highest potential for success for everyone at a reasonable cost. And that's how we approach it."

There is no arguing that CEF offers a valuable service to corporations looking for competent minority leadership. Peña points out that in 1988 the average score among the approximately 121,000 whites taking the Graduate Management Admissions Test was 508. Approximately 10,000 blacks took the same test, scoring an average of 387, while the 1,700 Hispanics who took it scored an average of 412. CEF demands that the minority candidates in their program meet the entrance requirements for Columbia and Stanford: The average score of students accepted into many of the top schools is 629.

But Peña is also realistic about the concerns participating corporations have when they agree to pair CEF Fellows with executive mentors. In addition to providing specific criteria for the selection of the mentor, "We ask the corporations to underwrite 60 percent of the Fellow's financial package," says Peña. "We think it's reasonable. Not all the corporations agree to do this, but most do. But corporations want to see their investments pay off. One company even told me, 'If after all this [the mentoring internship] is over, and we make an offer that is reasonable to the Fellow, we expect that individual to accept. And that will determine the extent to which we participate in the CEF program.' That attitude is unique. Some of the Fellows have been asked to return to the corporations where they were mentored. Some have gone back. Now, whether all of them go back or not is a different story. People in the CEF program are younger, more mobile, and more likely to take risks. Whether there is a high return of Fellows to the corporations will be one of the telling successes of the CEF program."

Eastman Kodak has sponsored two CEF Fellows so far, and according to Jack Murtz (interview by author, 1990) of Kodak's Professional Recruitment and University Development Department, the benefits to the organization of participating in such a program far outweigh the risks. Murtz says that while there is no commitment on the part of either the CEF Fellow or the company for long-term employment, Kodak sees itself contributing to the business community as a whole. "Even if they [the Fellows] don't become Kodak employees, we're developing high potential people for the future work force. And that's contributing to the industry in general," says Murtz. In addition, Kodak assigns the Fellows to real projects during the nine-month internship, so the protégés become an important resource for the company during the mentoring process. For example, one Fellow conducted focus-group discussions throughout the country as part of a market-research project.

Additional examples of the successes and difficulties with mentoring in industry, government, health care, nonprofit organizations, and education are cited throughout this and the remaining chapters. These examples eloquently attest to the fact that any organization—be it a large corporation or a small volunteer agency—must be aware of the positive and negative aspects of facilitated mentoring. It must be able to weigh the pros and cons and be willing to take the risks. Otherwise, such a program will never get off the ground, and if it does, it will likely be short-lived.

Benefits to the Organization

On the upside for the organization, consider the following positive points of facilitated mentoring:

Increased Productivity. A survey of twenty-four police officers in Kentucky who participated in a formal mentoring program revealed a significant tendency of the protégés to pick up the traits of discipline and hard work from their mentors (Fagan, 1986). Hard work generally means increased productivity. When protégés adopt this ethic from their mentors, you can tally a plus for facilitated mentoring.

Mentor/protégé relationships can also give a boost to productivity through performance planning and increased teamwork (Hogan, 1984). In the ideal facilitated mentoring program, the mentor, the protégé, and the protégé's natural boss plan projects and set standards for the protégé's performance. This teamwork approach, along with clear, measurable objectives for the protégé's performance, will typically increase the protégé's motivation and lead to superior performance and high productivity.

   Cost Effectiveness. One of the major benefits of facilitated mentoring programs is that they are cost-effective. In most programs, mentors carry out coaching responsibilities in addition to their regular job duties. (As Chapter Five makes clear, although mentoring often becomes just another part of the job, it is important to build in financial or other types of rewards for the mentor.) Similarly, protégés are expected to keep up individual job performance while participating in the mentor program, although most organizations allow some flexibility in scheduling and work load so that the protégé can meet with the mentor and complete related projects. And in good programs protégés' development activities are targeted to their specific needs. The protégés thus get highly relevant practice of needed skills without the cost of classroom training. With facilitated mentoring, there is no room to rent, no trainer to hire, and no excessive time off the job to compensate for.

   Improved Recruitment Efforts. General Electric's Power Generation Division has found mentoring to be a good training tool with an added plus. According to Louise O'Reilly (1989), manager of technical training, "We've also discovered that mentoring is a powerful concept in recruiting. Recognizing that the people we hire will be the future leaders of our company, we try to find the best students, develop them technically, and then continue to invest in them. Our college-campus interviewers impress upon the recruits that we just don't throw them into a difficult job and say good luck" (p. 4).
   This benefit holds true for educational organizations as well. In its mentoring program Trinity College in Washington, D.C., brings together student mentees (protégés) and accomplished alumni mentors who coach them in selected skills and experiences in preparation for their chosen careers. In a survey conducted by Kirby (1989, p. 5) all the respondents saw that the program "is good for the college; it shows that Trinity works." The program is a great success according to Mary Hayes, com-

mittee chair: "There is overwhelming interest by both potential mentors and students to keep the program going" (interview by author, 1990).

Mentoring can also be used to recruit new employees into fields that are not currently popular. For example, when the retail business was not considered as attractive a career option as banking or the legal profession, Jewel Tea used mentoring as a magnet. In the words of Franklin J. Lunding (Collins and Scott, 1978, p. 211), former chairman and chief executive officer, "We had to figure out ways of getting brains into the business. That's another way the 'first assistant' [a term they use for the mentor] philosophy helps the business; it attracts the smart ones."

Facilitated mentoring programs can thus make organizations appealing to potential employees, students, or affiliates. The first few days in any type of organization—whether it is a business, school, professional group, or volunteer agency—can be stressful. That stress is lessened when the mentor is there to guide the protégé through the unfamiliar maze. The anxious new employee can be reassured by the image the mentoring program conveys of a solid organization that takes care of its members.

Increased Organizational Communication and Understanding. The New York State Department of Taxation and Finance has offered cross-divisional mentoring to protégés since 1980. If the match is right, protégés can have mentors in offices across the state and in functional divisions different from their own. Mary Helen Rosenstein (interview by author, 1990), director of staff development and training, says that one of the real benefits of facilitated mentoring to her organization is that people in the districts get a perspective on how the central office in Albany operates. "Sometimes when the central office makes a decision, it may not make sense to people out in the district offices," says Rosenstein. "There are times when people in the district offices complain, 'Hey, Albany doesn't know what's happening here.' But a protégé from a district office who has a mentor in Albany begins to see that the central office has to make decisions based on many factors: the legislature's actions, requests from the governor's office, the needs of other divisions in the department, and so on. The protégé takes that information back to the district office. So the program has been a very good communication vehicle."

Maintenance of the Motivation of Senior People. "As the fires of his dreams and ambitions are banked, the mentor enjoys the stimulation of tutoring and guiding a younger person who is full of idealism and potential" (Groder, 1980, p. 5). Long-time employees, no matter how dedicated and loyal, sometimes lose their zeal for the job. Doing the same thing year after year — no matter how well it is done — is not a challenge. Senior people who participate as mentors can rethink their philosophies and methods, benefit from the fresh ideas of protégés, and see their own styles emulated in the organization. Stuart Hefter (interview by author, 1990), director of the Processing and Revenue Management Division of the New York State Department of Taxation and ten-year mentor, expresses it this way: "Why do I do it? I suppose self-satisfaction that I can do something for other people who will eventually succeed me. It's nice to know that there are people in the organization who think you can do something for their career and further their understanding; if they think that I can be of some assistance, I'm pleased to do that."

Enhancement of Services Offered by the Organization. It's no secret that human service agencies in the United States and many countries are facing a growing number of people in need. At the same time, the financial resources of many government and nonprofit agencies are shrinking. Facilitated mentoring is fast becoming a way to strengthen and enhance human service agencies. Pilot programs in San Antonio, Texas, and Stamford, Connecticut, are pairing community mentors with women on welfare to help them make the transition into the world of work. The YWCA's Project Redirection — a teenage pregnancy-prevention program — matches community women with teens who need emotional support and coaching on parenting skills. In such instances, facilitated mentoring is a win-win situation:

The organization's goals are furthered; clients get one-on-one assistance; caseworkers at the agencies can concentrate on managing and directing resources to the client; and mentors get a chance to be personally involved and make a positive difference in the lives of others.

Improvement in Strategic and Succession Planning. Typical long-range strategies for organizations include plans for market or operational areas, physical facilities, funding, and perhaps profits. Often they include staff projections based on anticipated growth and expected attrition. But these projections rarely include definite methods for recruiting, training, or promoting staff, although these considerations could easily make or break a growing organization. Many organizations assume that they will be able to hire or promote well-qualified people during periods of growth, that perfect employees will appear to fill vacant positions and will perform up to speed in no time at all. Training and development programs, particularly for managers or administrators at higher levels, are often given the lowest priority. Only when the performance of a group of employees is not meeting the expectations of top management do decision makers give serious attention to human-resource development in their strategic planning.

An organization with an effective mentoring program, however, can enhance strategic planning by providing a concrete way to move people into higher-level jobs. Improved succession planning and management development was one of the benefits of a formalized mentoring program cited by 42 percent of the respondents to a study carried out by PA Personnel Services (1986).

Such systematic succession planning is critical. When the planners in an organization make their people projections, they often find that many seasoned managers will be retiring in a few years. To shorten the typical development cycle of future leaders, they often consider a mentoring program. This concern sparked the mentoring program at Federal Express (Crosby, 1987). An officer in the Maintenance and Engineering Division became interested in developing successors within his division. He identified mentoring as a natural component of succession planning. Mentoring then became a career-development tool for management preceptors (protégés) in Federal Express's Leadership Institute.

Challenges for the Organization

In Chapter Two I mentioned that facilitated mentoring is not for everyone. It has limitations and risks just as all innovative programs do. Here are some of the negative, or downside, aspects of facilitated mentoring that organizations must consider.

Frustration. When there are few opportunities to move up in an organization, a facilitated mentoring program designed to support succession planning may not be a wise investment. People with high aspirations who see limited opportunity to advance are not likely to listen to a litany of the other benefits of facilitated mentoring. In fact, instituting a mentoring program may add to the frustration of ambitious managers who know there is little opportunity to advance and who see investment in this special program as a misuse of scarce resources.

Commitment. The success of facilitated mentoring programs depends on the organization's strong commitment to developing and promoting people from within. Organizations where this philosophy is not clearly evident probably should not consider facilitated mentoring. To many protégés, the implicit promise of mentoring is upward mobility in the organization. Jewel Tea makes good on this promise by setting a policy of early retirement, thus continually making room at the top for younger people. One Jewel executive expresses this belief: "This retirement program . . . is important in terms of opening up new opportunities" (Collins and Scott, 1978, p. 225).

Commitment is tested in other ways as well. From time to time, a protégé decides—as a result of close-up examination of values and developmental needs—to leave the company. This situation truly tests the commitment of the mentor and of the organization to people development: "A very talented individual who has gone as far as he can in our company," explains Crosby (1984, p. 2). "He is being groomed to someday take over a small corporation outside of our company. He and his mentor discuss global issues not directly related to internal company matters." This person continues to make a valued contribution to the company while he is there.

Financial and time commitments are further considerations. A mentoring program should be run for a minimum of three years to iron out the wrinkles and evaluate its effectiveness. It is unrealistic to expect to see results of any substantive development program in less than one year. It takes several months to get the structure in place and the mentor/protégé relationships established and running smoothly. In addition, time and money for tracking and evaluating the results with mentors, with protégés, and for the organization are necessary. "At some point in time, previously planned program goals should be formally evaluated to determine benefits for mentors, protégés, and the organization" (Gray, 1989, p. 21). The benefits of the program could also be quantified; however, that takes more work and money than a zealous cost cutter will probably want to approve.

The lack of true commitment to human-resource development is an overwhelming obstacle to the success of any training effort. Without strong support from the top decision makers, a mentoring program will not survive its first budget review, because the cost of such a special program will be all too obvious.

Coordination with Other Programs. A mentoring program typically supports or supplements other people-development programs in an organization. The CEF mentorships cited at the beginning of this chapter complement the MBA programs at Columbia and Stanford. In the New York State Department of Taxation, protégés can also take advantage of an internal public-administration training program. A company or agency with a large training department will usually find that mentoring strengthens existing programs by bridging the gap between classroom learning and real-world application. However, a lean organization, one that experiences many peak-and-valley work loads, probably does not have a large internal training and development department. Such an organization may find it cost-effective to use consultants as performance coaches.

There is another caution for organizations establishing facilitated mentoring as a separate, special program. Human-resource people are often, and understandably, jealous of their areas of responsibility for training and development programs. Objections to mentoring as a new or special program that "won't work here" may really be a symptom of turf protection. The key is to have all concerned participate in the planning process and to integrate the mentoring component with all the other components of human-resource development.

Hard to Sell. The lack of data on structured mentoring programs leads many decision makers to conclude that a formal program cannot be justified. There are few comprehensive studies of facilitated programs, probably because organizations do not take the time to analyze the results and publish reports of successful experiences. Also, it is difficult to isolate all the variables in order to make a direct correlation between a protégé's career success and mentoring. Because protégés typically seek out challenge and are ambitious and eager for self-improvement, determining whether they would have succeeded just as well without mentoring is a complicated task. In most cases, the best evidence that mentoring works is the praise of mentors and protégés who say that the mentoring experience was a benefit to both the organization and themselves.

In addition, mentoring can be difficult to describe to decision makers in an organization. Confusion about the roles and activities of mentors and protégés gives some cause for concern about the potential value of the mentoring process. It is sometimes much easier to talk about the magic or mystery of the experience than it is to describe exactly what takes place in the exchange. When the skills being taught to protégés are those of the crafts or trades, it is easy to describe the outcomes and to determine the investment for the organization. But when the skills are in management or administration, it is often difficult to measure the results and describe the mentor/protégé exchange. For example, one executive mentor explained that he simply let his protégés "get into my in-basket and see what's going on." Chapters Eight through Eleven give some useful descriptions of the roles and responsibilities of each person involved in a facilitated mentoring process.

Complicated and Expensive Administration. Cross-functional pairing requires extra coordination as well as an equal commitment to mentoring from the leaders of both departments. Geographical distances may produce other complications and expense because most interactions are by mail, telephone, or telefax, or involve travel. Time away from the job may make mentoring across functional areas too difficult to manage in some organizations. As cited previously, cross-functional pairing has been a clear benefit to the New York State Department of Taxation and Finance. For example, a protégé from the Audit Division has an opportunity to work with the Law Bureau, broadening the viewpoint of all people involved.

We have mentioned here only some of the benefits and risks for an organization considering facilitated mentoring. As you weigh the pros and cons, keep in mind the attributes of your organization: goals, size, growth, human resources programs, top-level attitudes, financial status. Chapter Seven describes how to determine the readiness of your organization and how to make your decision about the worth of facilitating mentoring there.

4

Payoffs and Penalties for the Protégé

Within days of taking up his position as assistant director of the Ogden, Utah, Service Center of the Internal Revenue Service (IRS), Steve Medlin faced a tough decision. Medlin had just completed a rigorous six-month period in the Executive Development (XD) Program of the IRS (interview by author, 1990). He was one of two outside applicants accepted into the highly structured program, which aims to develop candidates (protégés) with backgrounds in single functions into executives who make decisions based on multifunctional, or servicewide, needs. As part of the program, Medlin talked with scores of IRS executives and attended regular meetings with a coach (mentor), who focused on his individual needs and concerns.

Still, after six months of being immersed in the workings and politics of the IRS, Medlin had some doubts about his own executive abilities. After all, he had not done any hands-on decision making; he had not proved himself in the organization. But when his managers brought him the following problem, he had to put those doubts aside. A clerk had a long-standing debt on a student loan, and a collection agency had come calling for payment. The IRS has a policy that employees must have their financial houses in order. Medlin's managers recommended that the clerk be fired: Policy is policy. But Medlin had learned in the XD Program that the IRS also embraces an important value:

respect for the individual. After considering the clerk's case, he decided to give her time to make good on the loan. She did.

"What I realized," says Medlin, "is that the XD Program provided me with tremendous exposure to the IRS, its value system and its culture. I saw how other executives use those things to make decisions. In regard to personnel issues, I learned how the IRS feels about people and treats people. So when it came right down to it, I had the skills I needed to make a good decision." Medlin's case is a good example of the potential payoffs that facilitated mentoring offers protégés: skills, self-confidence, and the ability to take risks.

Benefits for the Protégé

The benefits discussed by Alleman (1982) and Zey (1984) are summarized by the American Society for Training and Development (1986) as follows:

- Performance and productivity ratings are higher for protégés than for nonprotégés.
- Protégés are paid more, take more pleasure in their work, and have greater career satisfaction than nonprotégés.
- Protégés have more knowledge of the technical and organizational aspects of the business than nonprotégés.

Here is a close look at the most striking payoffs for protégés who participate in facilitated mentoring programs.

Targeted Development Activities. What typically happens when a person's skill deficiencies surface through self-perception, a supervisor's appraisal, or some other form of assessment? Quite often a training course or seminar is found or designed to fill the person's needs. Such courses may or may not provide the person with the exact skills, knowledge, and practice needed to become a good performer.

In good facilitated mentoring programs, however, interested parties produce a development plan that addresses the exact needs of the protégé. In most businesses, this development plan is formulated by the protégé, the mentor, the protégé's natural boss, and the program coordinator, who identify specific ways to develop the protégé's skills. Not only are they likely to match training or practice to the need, but accountability is built into the process by having all four parties agree on the processes to be pursued.

Wells Fargo Bank (R. Addison, interview by author, 1989) used this skills-based approach when it developed its Branch Manager MAP (meaning a guide; MAP is not an acronym) program. Skills needed to perform branch manager functions were identified, and activities were then selected that would promote the development of those skills. For example, the branch manager can be required to read policies and answer questions, talk with model bank employees, or complete a self-study course in communication. As part of the program, each branch manager is also assigned a MAP manager—a higher-level executive who can waive or add to these developmental activities based on the employee's needs and performance—who functions as a mentor. The MAP manager gives support and direction to the branch manager, providing key information on the culture and inner workings of the organization that could never be gained in a general training class.

Increased Likelihood of Success. Charlie Hartness, a popular and valued mentor (now retired) among the managers at Federal Express, comments (quoted in Avant and Crosby DeBerry, 1985), "Simply avoiding failure is not all that it takes to be successful. I think probably the most important contribution a mentor can make to candidates is helping them to avoid failure. They will succeed on the basis of their own competencies, as long as they avoid failing in the process."

This philosophy that fewer failures increase the likelihood of success is causing mentoring to become an important educational tool, particularly for at-risk youth. At the 1990 National Mentoring Conference, presentations were made on the use of mentoring to maximize the expertise of mentor teachers and to increase retention rates of blacks and other minority students. Project Literacy U.S. (PLUS) is engineering a mentoring project called "One PLUS One." Its goal is to promote formal mentoring to further literacy, academic achievement, career goals, and self-esteem in young people. Lauro F. Cavazos, U.S. Secretary of Education (1990, p. 1), states, "The risks that all young people face are compounded for those who are poor, members of racial or ethnic minorities, or recent immigrants. These youths often attend the weakest schools, have fewer successful adult role models, . . . and have the fewest clearly visible paths to opportunities in the mainstream. For these youngsters, studies are finding that those who receive support from a mature, caring adult—a mentor—are more likely to finish high school and more likely to hold a job. These are significant behavior changes, and necessary ones, because we as a society cannot afford to allow our children to fail. Their failures are not only personal tragedies but also direct threats to our national standard of living and our democratic institutions."

This current trend in the educational world provides an important lesson for the business sector: Mentoring can be equally important to the problem employee and the high potential one. Groder (1980) describes the promising young employee who, though bright and creative, misses deadlines and does sloppy work. He suggests that the young person be matched with a mentor who can give help and direction. The unproductive employee may find a supporter and role model in a mentor, someone to assist in bringing about small successes that lead to big behavior change.

Less Time Spent in the Wrong Position. "I'm bored. My skills aren't being used. I feel like I have nowhere to go. I'm tracked into a career path I didn't want to be in. The only way for me to make more money is to move into management, but I don't want to be a manager." So goes the lament of employees who are not able to match their interests with the organization's needs. They spend their work days in misery and dissatisfaction until they quit, feeling that they have wasted their time in a career or organization they didn't care about.

Traditionally, organizations have assumed the responsibility for planning the career paths of employees. Someone up there decides when to train, when to reassign, and when to promote employees at all levels. In many accounting firms, for example, the junior auditor is moved to auditor to senior auditor to manager to partner. It is assumed that the employee will go up or go out. In one organization in which I worked there was a secret "ready now" binder that included profiles on managers who were targeted for movement in the company. Often the first clue one had of being in the binder was a request to have a professional photograph taken! This ready-made career ladder can appeal to an employee, but in many such cases career goal setting follows the assignment rather than preceding it. Employees who accept this approach often feel that someone is playing puppeteer with the strings of their lives, yanking them this way and that to fit the current needs of the organization. The result can be apathy, dependency, frustration, stress, job burnout, and the loss of independent-minded employees who would prefer to integrate their own values and ambitions with those of the organization — truly a high price.

What can facilitated mentoring do to aid these valuable employees who feel stuck? First, facilitated mentoring provides a pathway for those who want to walk to meet their luck. In such a program protégés serve their own interests by participating in setting goals and creating action plans to attain them. Quite often this activity pays off in tangible ways. In its summary, the American Society for Training and Development (1986) claims that protégés achieve executive level two years before those who have not been involved in a mentoring relationship.

Second, mentors can direct people to positions in the organization that match their interests and skills. In such cases, skillful mentors can save the organization costly turnovers.

Third, caring and informed mentors can help people avoid careers that are unsuitable. Educational mentoring programs can keep youths out of jobs that are inappropriate and that would lead to failure. In an interesting twist, many college students in teacher-training programs are offered the option of becoming mentors for high school youth. If these teacher candidates (protégés) are unable to demonstrate promise as mentors, they are then advised by their own mentors to find suitable careers! In industry, employees are sometimes mentored to leave the company eventually. One such situation is described by Crosby (1984, p. 2) as benefiting everyone involved, even the company: "We realize we can't offer him everything, but in the meanwhile, during the three to five years the process takes, the company is benefiting from his productivity and enthusiasm."

Pygmalion Effect. Dione Gomez was lazy and she knew it. That's why she asked George Curry, New York bureau chief for the *Chicago Tribune*, to be her mentor. When Gomez began procrastinating about writing news stories, Curry wrote what he described as a blistering letter. "Basically I told her to put up or shut up," Curry says (interview by author, 1990) in his endearing way. Gomez (interview by author, 1990) is more complimentary. "Basically, George said he thought I had potential. He told me 'I think you can do well. I have faith in you. I think you have potential, and I think you can get it together.' And I did. Now he introduces me to his colleagues as his first mentee in New York. He's proud of me, and it feels great." Gomez has since had several front-page stories in publications, and she plans one day to have a job much like Curry's.

This story illustrates an interesting payoff for protégés. Bosses, teachers, even parents often expect people to perform just the way they have all along. But a mentor has fewer biases about what someone has done in the past and tends to see potential that no one else does. The mentor can create the expectation that the protégé will do more and do it better than before. And, just like Eliza Doolittle with the tutoring of Professor Higgins, the protégé achieves well because both parties expect that. A powerful mentor also reflects power on a protégé. The visibility of the relationship sends a signal to others that the protégé has access to the resources and power of the mentor.

Increased Awareness of the Organization. When the protégé has a mentor at a higher level in the organization, important information is passed on in their discussions. This communication is likely to be more effective, and certainly more timely, than company newsletters or management bulletins. The protégé who knows the future direction of the organization can design career plans accordingly and can focus development activities on the changing requirements of the business. For example, when companies converted mechanical and electrical equipment and devices to electronic ones, many engineers found their skills obsolete. Had they known ahead of time about this shift in direction, those who were motivated to stay with the companies could have pursued training in electronics.

Awareness of other industries, professions, or careers is a potential benefit when a mentor is outside the protégé's current organization. These different-organization relationships are not often designed as facilitated mentoring programs, yet many people have described to us great value accruing to them from such a relationship.

Possible Pitfalls for the Protégé

Mentoring does not always work out in the protégé's favor; sometimes it can lead to problems and frustrating experiences. Here are some potential pitfalls to consider.

Expectation That Protégé Will Neglect Core Job. Let's face it. Some managers and supervisors are convinced that subordinates are out to cheat the company. For example, many supervisors continue to resist flextime work schedules, although studies show they result in increased productivity and job satisfaction. Apparently this resistance is an indicator of their concern that people will not work without close supervision. It is fairly common to hear managers express the concern that development activities suggested by the mentor will be so attractive and engrossing that the employee will neglect the routine job. And, undoubtedly, a protégé who is not ready for self-management will sometimes slip through the most careful screening processes. But there is overwhelming evidence that such a person is the exception to the rule. When people feel that intelligent consideration is given to their growth and development, they often exert great effort to perform in all aspects of the job.

Expectation That Protégé Will Play Mentor Against Boss. True, if the relationship between the boss and the subordinate is not a good one, the subordinate will reach out to the mentor for positive interaction. This is a good reason to include the boss as well as the mentor in development planning. Such an arrangement helps diffuse subversive behavior and makes the roles and responsibilities of everyone involved in the mentoring relationship crystal clear. Chapters Eight, Nine, and Ten give specifics on how the roles of the mentor, protégé, and boss can be structured to maximize harmony in this triangle.

Having Unrealistic Expectations About Promotion. People in one organization that I worked with would not use the term *candidate* for the protégé because they felt it implied promotion as a result of participation in the program. However, in some mentoring programs, especially federal government executive-development programs, those who complete the activities successfully and meet clearly stated criteria will be promoted. In other programs, it is understood that while being a protégé can enhance one's chances for promotion, it is not a guarantee. In the New York State Department of Taxation and Finance, for example, protégés must still pass the same written and oral civil-service tests as their nonprotégé colleagues before even being considered for promotion. To forestall unrealistic expectations on the part of protégés, it is important to clearly communicate to all what participation in the program means—and what it does not mean.

Being Unable to Take Responsibility for Own Development. While interviewing people for this book, I heard the following problems about protégés from program coordinators (along with their solutions):

• "The mentors sometimes say the protégés aren't assertive enough. So we give them that feedback and tell them to get on the phone and contact their mentors."

- "Some of them lack people skills. We're looking into getting some of them into communication classes so they can make better use of the relationship."
- "When they first take responsibility for developing their own studies, they are full of anxiety. But as time goes on, they become more relaxed. They know how to take on responsibility and find their way around."

These three examples of protégé shortcomings indicate that it is indeed sometimes a problem for protégés to become responsible for their own development. But practice, feedback, and formal intervention can make a difference. It takes work to unlearn dependent behavior, and because of that, facilitated mentoring programs do not operate without problems. They can have built-in mechanisms such as careful coordination and evaluation to make adjustments and to enable protégés to take responsibility for their own development.

Being the Object of Jealousy and Gossip. People capable enough to get into prestigious business schools and executive-development programs are often labeled by less gifted colleagues as teachers' pets or, worse yet, brown-nosers. However, most ambitious, self-motivated people will occasionally get those comments whether they are in a facilitated mentoring program or not. One protégé whose informal mentor was two levels above her voiced the opinion that a facilitated mentoring program would have actually prevented the jealousy and gossip that she experienced. A structured program would have clearly defined the relationship, making it legitimate and less suspicious in her co-workers' eyes.

Having a Mentor Who Does Not Keep Commitments. "I was lucky. My coach [mentor] was good. But some of the other people in the program had coaches who were worthless. They didn't think it was politically wise to ask for a different coach. So they stuck it out. But they didn't learn anything" (confidential protégé interview by author, 1990). Sometimes mentors do not keep time commitments. Sometimes they do not assist the protégé with developmental activities. And unless there is intervention on the part of a coordinator, the protégé will be penalized by the relationship rather than rewarded.

It is crucial to screen and orient and evaluate mentors. Guidelines for the mentor recruitment and selection process are detailed in Chapter Eight. Those who accept the mentor role must know that the primary reason for the relationship is to develop skills and experience in the protégé systematically. Both protégés and mentors must be evaluated and given feedback during the process in order to make the best of the relationship.

In addition, the relationship must be based on a negotiated agreement that includes at the minimum:

- The explicit description of skills to be learned and practiced
- The types of activities that will provide this practice
- Agreements on time and frequency of meetings and feedback sessions

When a mentor does not follow the negotiated agreement, clear guidelines must describe how the situation can be handled. The protégé must feel comfortable going to the program coordinator and asking for third-party intervention. This issue is addressed in Chapter Twelve.

Having a Mentor Who Takes Credit for the Protégé's Work. Every organization has a few unethical people who may take advantage of the unsuspecting. To protect protégés from this possible penalty, it is a good idea to make mentor/protégé projects public. Some programs feature bimonthly meetings chaired by the coordinator in which both the mentor and the protégé discuss project progress and outline their contributions. In such meetings, skillful coordinator counseling and peer influence can prevent the mentor from taking undue credit for the protégé's work.

Once again, part of the process for the protégé will be learning to interact successfully with many different types of managers, good ones and bad. If protégés feel exploited, they must be willing and able to approach their coordinators for help. The coordinators can then coach the protégés on strategies for working out satisfactory agreements with the mentors.

People who are interested in becoming protégés must take time to consider the potential payoffs and possible penalties. Those who go into mentoring relationships expecting instant magic will soon be disappointed. The best of relationships demand communication and problem-solving skills. A protégé who enters a relationship with open eyes and realistic expectations will more than likely get the payoffs he or she is looking for.

5

The Mentor's Motivation and Concerns

Keith Elkins likes mentoring so much, he does it full-time. Elkins is a professor at Empire State College in New York, where all faculty are considered mentors (interview by author, 1990). Typically, Elkins holds individual meetings with each of his full-time students about once a week and each of his half-time students about once every two weeks. Together they draft learning contracts and discuss learning strategies. Each student must come up with an individualized curriculum for obtaining a degree. Elkins's job is to guide and aid the student in any way he can.

"In our initial meeting, I ask the new student three basic questions," says Elkins. "'What do you want to study? Why do you want to study that? How do you learn best?' Sometimes I may sound contentious, but it makes the student think."

Elkins and the student then decide on activities and assignments, which are usually completed on an individual basis. There are no formal lectures or labs at Empire State (H. Hammett, interview by author, 1990). The student is responsible for designing and completing his or her own educational plan and must help seek out resources to do so. Mentors like Elkins are the student's most vital resource. The Empire State College program is a unique part of the State University of New York system. It is facilitated mentoring at an extreme. Obviously, it works for only the most motivated students—and the most dedicated mentors.

Elkins was initially drawn to the program in 1975 because it fit his own "John Dewey-like" philosophy of education. Now, he sees the costs of such a program. It requires massive amounts of paperwork and coordination on the part of the mentors. Yet Elkins and many of his well-qualified co-workers are not seeking greener academic pastures. What makes them stay? After a bit of thought, Elkins answers. "It sounds a bit self-serving," he says, "but I guess we're just a bunch of cockamamie idealists. This program, even though it's demanding, comes the closest to what we believe education should be. This is a very rewarding place." Indeed. The lesson is that a carefully structured mentoring program—whether in a large corporation or a small volunteer organization—will reward and hence motivate good mentors in many ways.

Benefits for the Mentor

Here are some of the key personal and professional motivators a facilitated program can offer mentors.

Enhanced Self-Esteem. Imagine being asked by a less-experienced person to be his or her mentor! The request suggests that you are respected, admired, and noticed in the organization. Mary Helen Rosenstein, who helps manage the mentor program at the New York State Department of Taxation (interview by author, 1990), explains that although mentors there participate on a strictly voluntary basis, they must be specifically requested by a protégé before a match is made. "This type of recognition helps the way mentors see themselves," says Rosenstein. "There's a bit of an ego thing going on here, and it's good for the mentor." Observing that others are being requested to function as mentors may be a stimulus to other managers to sharpen their own skills and images.

Revitalized Interest in Work. To the open-minded mentor, a protégé can be a breath of fresh air. Preston Munter, professor of psychiatry at Harvard Law School (Hughes, 1980), believes that in many mentoring relationships the mentor exchanges wisdom for the protégé's creative energy. A protégé can stimulate the mentor's thinking in new ways about subjects the mentor considered stale.

"Mentors may actually get more out of the activity than their protégés," says Suzanne Robinson (1990), manager of management development for Planning Research Corporation. "Senior managers [mentors] have clearer ideas about what they are learning from the experience" of meeting several hours a month over a one-year period with their protégés (p. 6).

Close Relationship with the Protégé. I have suggested that many opponents of facilitated mentoring see it as an artificial relationship. However, closeness can develop in a facilitated program. One mentor at Trinity College described her relationship with her protégé this way: "We just talk about things and enjoy them and laugh together. We both thought we had to be real serious, but then [en route to an event together] we began to laugh about all this. When we get together, we tell Trinity stories and just funny things that have happened" (quoted in Kirby, 1989, p. 20).

Closeness doesn't always occur, yet it can be a side benefit. Marilyn Zuckerman, an AT&T quality-planning manager, says, "The mentor is there to deal on an emotional level, . . . to impart a greater sense of purpose and to be encouraging" (1990, p. 6).

Financial Reward. Some programs provide financial rewards for mentors. In many police departments, Field Training Officers (Fagan, 1989) typically receive a 5 percent pay differential for mentoring, coaching, and evaluating the performance of new cadets on a regular basis over a three- to six-month period. In other organizations, the mentor may receive a promotion or bonus if performance is judged satisfactory.

Fulfillment of Own Developmental Needs. For executives who want to leave a particular legacy in an organization, facilitated mentoring is a way for them to do so. Reich (1985) conducted a study of 520 executives in the Columbia University Executive

Program. Participants included decision makers at all levels—presidents, vice-presidents, general managers, and managers—of major corporations. Some were mentors; others were protégés. According to Reich (p. 17), "Being a mentor for high performers was satisfying to most executives. As psychologist Erik Erikson pointed out, middle-aged people want to leave part of themselves to the next generation, and this dynamic may be a large part of the mentoring process. The essence of these relationships was captured in some of the executives' statements: 'I am committed to the development of younger people. But this is self-motivated, not company directed.'"

Professional Assistance on Work Projects. In many facilitated programs, the protégé completes projects under the mentor's guidance and is thus an added resource for the mentor. One mentor who developed several protégés in his organization stated that he tries to keep the best ones in his division. In Reich's study (1985, p. 44), "Mentors (75–90 percent) highly valued being able to keep high flyers on their team and thus improve group performance."

Halatin (1989, p. 27) neatly summarizes the major benefits to the mentor in this way.

> The supervisor or employee who is a mentor enjoys the intrinsic satisfaction of helping another work toward his or her goals. It is a special moment for the mentor when a subordinate achieves something toward which he or she has worked. The mentor is also able to experience a feeling of self-importance from the respect given by the subordinate, the interest shown in the mentor's stories of past successes, and the treatment of his or her advice by the employee as action guidelines and principles. The respect and appreciation for past efforts by the mentor can lead to a lasting relationship between the two individuals. Through the mentoring relationship itself, mentors can gain information about the organization and operations.

Subordinates are natural resources, often willing and eager to share their knowledge. The additional contribution to the organization and its members made as a mentor can also be important to the mentor at evaluation time. Noted will be his or her contribution to the creation of a team spirit within the organization.

Concerns for Mentors

Of course, being a mentor can have its downside too. Some programs actually have demotivating factors that test the most altruistic of mentors. The following discussion looks at some of these issues and provides workable suggestions to organizations for eliminating obstacles or at least minimizing them.

Pressure to Take on the Mentoring Role. A facilitated mentoring program typically recognizes mentors as special, thus making the role an attractive one to people who are capable and want to maintain good standing in the organization. When mentors get added recognition, other managers may feel pressured to volunteer, whether they are suited to the role or not.

A good facilitated program must screen mentor candidates carefully. The manager who prefers spreadsheets to a one-on-one conversation must be counseled by the program coordinator. A good coordinator can help the potential mentor see alternative routes to promotion or recognition in the organization. Unwillingness to screen out inappropriate mentor candidates will result in frustration on the part of the unsuitable mentor and the protégé.

Lack of Requisite Skills. Chapter One described some of the characteristics and skills required of mentors. For example, the mentor must be able to tutor, give feedback, do career planning, and assist the protégé in specific activities. It is possible that a mentor candidate lacks a critical skill, say the ability to plan a career path, but is excellent in other ways. Because this person is understandably reluctant to reveal the lack of knowledge or skills, tactful measurement of specific skills is a necessary, although complex, task. Strategies can then be used to build the missing skills in suitable candidates. In our example, the potential mentor can be scheduled to participate in an orientation program that includes information on career planning. In addition, the coordinator must be willing to act as a resource and be able to coach when the mentor is not performing satisfactorily.

Not Taking the Coaching and Feedback Role Seriously. Coaching is at the core of the mentoring process. What exactly is coaching? The mentor must be able to direct the protégé to relevant activities and projects. The mentor must be able to say what is going well and where more practice is needed. The mentor must be able to differentiate competent from not yet competent behaviors of the protégé. That discrimination suggests that the observed performance is assessed against some standard, which is a functional definition of appraisal—letting people know how they are doing relevant to an agreed standard. For feedback to be most effective it must be based on objective appraisal, include positive reinforcement of desired behaviors, and provide modeling of or instruction on those behaviors to be improved. "Feedback encourages people to control their own work, and work for self-administered approval" (Odiorne, 1985, p. 66). Mastery of appraisal, coaching, and feedback skills is essential and fundamental to this task. If there is any question about the strengths of a potential mentor in these key areas, some form of training in coaching and feedback must be included in the orientation.

The protégé can also influence the quality of the coaching and feedback by asking the mentor for assistance in specific tasks. For example, if the protégé is to make a major presentation to a prospective client, the protégé may ask the mentor to listen to a practice session and give some pointers on how to handle potentially troublesome parts of the talk. Further, the protégé may ask the mentor to sit in on the presentation and give feedback at a later time. This committed interaction, initiated by the protégé, is highly likely to be taken seriously by both the protégé and the mentor.

In addition, organizational procedures can influence the mentor role. When the mentor's ability to coach is appraised regularly, the mentor will take the coaching responsibility seriously.

Lacking Time to Work with Protégés. Many experienced managers and administrators cite the development of others as their primary responsibility. When one top-level executive was asked how he fit meetings with a protégé into his work schedule, he answered, "I'm always mentoring, both formally and informally. My role is to help my subordinates make decisions. I let them bounce ideas off me and I give my input. But ultimately, I want them to be able to make their own decisions. If I were making all their decisions for them, I wouldn't need them, would I? So taking on what you call an 'additional protégé' is no great hardship for me in terms of time. It's what I do anyway" (S. Hefter, interview by author, 1990).

Not all managers have this philosophy. Some managers who assume the mentor role become so busy with their own work that they give the protégé interaction low priority. When there is a time crunch, the first meeting canceled is the one with the protégé.

This attitude can be countered if the mentor's time with the protégé is linked to performance appraisal and if the coordinator tracks meeting times and frequencies. The program must help the mentor make time with the protégé a high priority. With regular feedback, mentors can learn to use their time creatively to meet regular work demands and the needs of the protégé. Depending on the nature of the formal agreement, face-to-face meetings with the protégé may be on a monthly basis with telephone contact in between. The mentor who feels put upon to keep appointments must remember that the protégé is taking the initiative to complete extra work assignments; the mentor has the easier, less time-consuming role.

Also, mentors can turn the protégé into their own time-saving resource by delegating meaningful work to the protégé.

This strategy serves a dual purpose. It frees up time for the mentor while developing the protégé's work skills. Delegated tasks that are a challenge offer a substantive experience for the protégé (Murray-Hicks, 1987).

No Perceived Reward, Benefit, or Payoff. Lack of rewards for the mentor is one of the most commonly mentioned obstacles to structuring the mentoring process. Dynamic, impatient leaders will let you know quickly that there must be something visible in it for them if they are to make a significant time and energy investment in a function that primarily benefits others. A mentor with little motivation may simply drop out of the job.

As noted, some mentors will be amply rewarded by the knowledge that they are contributing to the growth and development of another person. Other mentors need concrete rewards to sustain their involvement. In either case, people tend to repeat those activities that result in some reward, and therefore, even though it takes some effort and creativity, rewards for the mentors can and must be designed into the program.

The importance of making mentoring part of performance appraisal has already been discussed at length. Professional recognition of a good job should be included in the mentor's regular progress reviews. At 3M the mentor role itself is a reward, a role that is earned and respected (3M Report, 1989). In other organizations, promotions or financial advancement are a direct outcome of the effort spent in mentoring. For example, in California, teachers in some school districts can earn up to $70,000 by agreeing to be mentors. In industry bonus points may be awarded for sustained successful performance as a mentor.

Another way to reward mentors is through public recognition. If your organization has a newsletter or periodical you might include a "Mentor of the Month" story. Examples of particularly noteworthy assistance can be gathered from the protégés. Publicity about the program can also include biographical sketches of or statements from people who serve as mentors. This public recognition of competence and leadership can be a powerful reward.

Possessiveness of Protégés. Occasionally a mentor will identify so strongly with a protégé that he or she becomes jealous and possessive. The mentor then undermines the interaction between the natural boss and the protégé. The mentor who competes for the attention and time of the protégé, emphasizing the priority of their relationship over the protégé's regular work duties, creates a divisive situation. When the protégé gets caught up in making comparisons between the mentor and the boss, and the boss loses, the whole situation deteriorates.

Several techniques can be used to keep the mentor's perspective in line. First, a negotiated agreement between the protégé, mentor, and natural boss must clearly outline the work expected of the protégé. If the protégé is to perform all regular duties during the mentoring relationship, emphasizing this expectation in the agreement helps to invest the mentor in the protégé's regular work assignment. Second, the duration of the relationship must be stated in the agreement. The mentor will then be aware of the finite nature of the formal relationship. Finally, it is of the utmost importance to keep communication channels open between the protégé, the protégé's natural boss, the mentor, and the coordinator. If possessiveness surfaces, the mentor must be reminded of the purpose of the relationship.

Not Letting Protégé Take the Risks Necessary for Learning. When the mentor has a strong vested interest in the protégé's success, the mentor may also be tempted to take on some of the protégé's tasks. If a project is highly visible, the mentor may want the protégé to look good for the mentor's sake and overstep the fine line between guidance and doing work for the protégé. There is some element of risk in most learning situations but experience is in fact the best teacher. In orientation and feedback sessions, mentors must be reminded that guided learning can increase the likelihood of success for the protégé and enhance the protégé's self-esteem. It is the mentor's role to guide and advise—not to do.

Resentment of Protégé. A subordinate who openly expresses the desire to learn, grow, and advance in the organization may be a threat to a manager who is at the next higher level. For this reason, managers sometimes ignore the potential of a direct subordinate or, worse yet, throw obstacles in the subordinate's path.

A relatively easy way to avoid this pitfall in a facilitated program is to match the protégé with a mentor who is at least two levels higher.

In flatter organizations this solution may not be possible. But additional distance can be engineered by matching mentors with protégés in different departments or functions. Yvonne Shepard, a mentor at AT&T Bell Laboratories (1989), finds that having a protégé from a different department helps her to bring an objectivity to the relationship that a supervisor might not have.

If you are thinking about becoming a mentor or if you are structuring a facilitated program, review the following summary of what makes it matter for the mentor.

- Refined interpersonal skills. Mentors hone their own skills for effective interaction with others.
- Self-esteem enhanced; psychic rewards; pride in helping others to grow. The experience of helping another to grow instills pride in the helper.
- Enhanced status in the organization. Mentors are respected for the valuable role they play in the development of future leaders of the organization.
- Job enrichment with unusual projects. In a stable or downsizing organization, a mentor who has mastered the job will find enrichment in projects that are outside usual responsibilities.
- Additional work accomplished.
- Career advancement. The mentor may get promoted because of effective people development.
- Financial rewards. Bonuses or other financial incentives may be given to those who take on the extra task of mentoring.
- Creative input for ongoing work.
- Avoidance of burnout due to routine work or overwork.

- Maintenance of motivation when on a plateau. The fresh viewpoint of the protégé may renew the enthusiasm and motivation of the mentor.
- Public recognition and acclaim. Publicity about the existence and effectiveness of the mentoring program provides added recognition of the stature of the mentor.
- Extended influence on the mission and direction of the organization.

If you are still interested in a facilitated program after reviewing the benefits and the possible downside for mentors, go on to Part Two for the how-tos.

Facilitated Mentoring: How to Make It Work

Part Two describes mentoring programs in several different types of organizations. Illustrations of the key components of each program are included in Chapter Six. The activities that take place in each component are described only briefly there, but are discussed in detail in Chapters Eight through Thirteen.

Models and Applications

Figure 1 in Chapter Six presents a generic model that includes most of the essential activities one would encounter in a facilitated mentoring program. Figures 2 through 7 in that chapter illustrate six other models, each of which applies to a specific organization. These programs have been in operation from one year to ten years. Objectives for each are stated.

Model Number 1 (Figure 1)

Generic model for a facilitated program. Developed by Murray-Hicks (1972).

Model Number 2 (Figure 2)

Executive Candidate Development Program (ECDP) in the U.S. General Accounting Office (GAO). The GAO has approximately 5,100 people on staff, with 125 at the senior executive level. Fifty to sixty candidates apply for the ECDP each year.

Model Number 3 (Figure 3)

Public-sector mentoring program (organization identity confidential). Small, specialized group in a federal agency with a need to prepare successors for a function that requires a high degree of skills and independent responsibility.

Model Number 4 (Figure 4)

Rooney, Ida, Nolt and Ahern, Certified Public Accountants — member of Midsnell International — is a full-service public accounting firm headquartered in Oakland, California. There are approximately 100 persons on the professional staff.

Model Number 5 (Figure 5)

Trinity College Mentoring Program in Washington, D.C. The primary goal of the program is to offer selected student mentees (protégés) the opportunity to work with a mentor in a professional area related to her academic major or career interests.

Model Number 6 (Figure 6)

Tumor Registrars Association of California (TRAC). Application of a facilitated mentor program in the field of health care, pairing hospital-based professionals with association volunteers. In 1985 the state of California passed a mandatory reporting law requiring all new cancer cases be reported by certified tumor registrars. The objective of the mentoring program is to increase the level of productivity in the tumor registries and the quality of care provided to patients.

Model Number 7 (Figure 7)

Empire State College in New York. Since 1971 the faculty has been designated as "mentor" to define a new role in higher education. The mentor program objective is to have mentors and students develop learning contracts for guided, individualized studies that lead to undergraduate degrees.

How to Make It Work

After you have reviewed each of the models, you will be familiar with most of the processes associated with facilitated mentoring programs. Our research and experience prove that with careful design, administration, and evaluation, facilitated mentoring programs can maximize benefits and minimize risks in the right organizations. What is the right organization? Chapter Seven will help you answer that question.

Chapters Eight through Thirteen describe the nuts and bolts of facilitated mentoring programs. These chapters cover all the components of the generic model presented in Figure 1. Each of these chapters ends with a checklist of the key factors influencing implementation of the component discussed in the chapter. Use the checklists to jot down ideas that will help you prepare for successful implementation.

Issues

In many of the workshops we do on facilitated mentoring, we ask people to finish the sentence: "It won't work here because. . . ." This exercise generates many concerns, most of which have been dealt with in this book already. But other, sensitive issues also come up. Don't mentors and protégés often fall in love? If the program is only for women and minorities, aren't we risking alienating our other employees? Will their jealousy fuel racism? How do unions react to such programs? Chapter Fourteen attempts to answer questions like these and to describe practical ways to approach issues such as the relationship between the mentor and protégé, and management and organizational issues.

6

Mentoring Models and Applications

In Part One you read about the many benefits and the most likely problems for organizations, for mentors, and for protégés when the mentoring process is facilitated. To realize fully the beneficial results of facilitating the mentoring process, it is important to implement a program designed to function successfully and to avoid problems. Preventive actions and remedies for pitfalls can help guarantee a smooth, successful program most of the time. Figure 1 illustrates a generic model that contains the major components of a good mentoring program. Other applications and variations of mentoring programs are illustrated in Figures 2 through 7. If you are considering a facilitated mentoring program or just want to learn how a good one works, scanning these illustrations is the place to start. This chapter tells only what is taking place in each program. The following chapters give details on how to implement a program and manage each of these components in your organization.

Generic Model for a Facilitated Mentoring Program

Figure 1 illustrates a comprehensive facilitated mentoring program that can be implemented in many different types and sizes of organizations. Each of the components is described briefly here.

Figure 1. Generic Model for a Facilitated Mentoring Program.

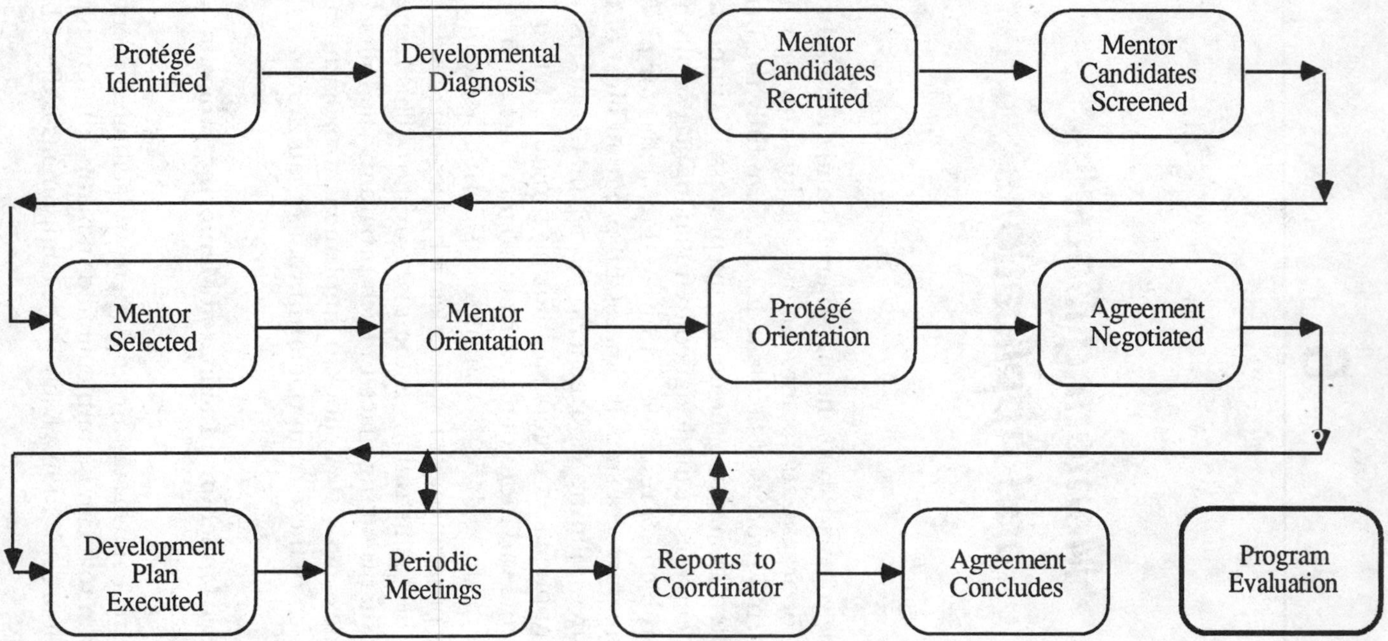

Source: Adapted from Murray-Hicks, 1972.

Protégé Identified   In this step, the organization identifies the group of people who are eligible for the mentoring program—for example, by targeting women in supervisory production jobs who can be groomed to move into management positions. One program identified its target group as minorities at the second level of management. Other examples are candidates for senior executive positions or any new employee who wants to take advantage of such developmental assistance. Individual protégés may volunteer, may be nominated by a boss or other sponsor, or may compete for selection through application and testing. The protégé's identity and agreement to participate can be entered into a record or database for tracking the results of the mentoring effort.

Developmental Diagnosis   In this step, the developmental needs of the protégé are determined and some form of individual development plan is prepared. The diagnosis may be as simple as the self-perception of the protégé. For cxample, "I need to learn more about project planning and cost estimating." Or the diagnosis may be as sophisticated as a formal two-week assessment with elaborate simulations of real-world situations observed by trained assessors. In-between these two extremes are such possibilities as having bosses determine developmental needs or having skill deficiencies revealed through easy-to-use assessment instruments. Ideally, development needs will be ranked in order of priority.

Mentor Candidates Recruited	This step produces the individuals who will function as mentors. They may volunteer for the role, may be chosen by a protégé, or may be recruited by senior managers.
Mentor Candidates Screened	Volunteers or draftees for the mentor positions are screened and prequalified by a coordinator or administrator of the program or by a panel or advisory board. At this point the general ability and willingness of the mentor are assessed.
Mentor Selected	A mentor is selected for a specific protégé after consideration of the skills and knowledge wanted by the protégé and the ability of the mentor to provide practice or guidance in those areas. Compatibility of styles and personalities can also be a factor in the selection.
Mentor Orientation	The most eager and competent mentor must still be oriented to the role. Time commitments, types of activities, time and budget support, relationship with the natural boss, and reporting requirements are some typical subjects covered in the mentor orientation.
Protégé Orientation	An explicit orientation can get the protégé off to a good start too. The subjects included in this session can be similar to those covered in the mentor orientation. Other topics to consider are assertiveness training and career planning.
Agreement Negotiated	A clear agreement is an essential foundation of a good mentor/protégé

relationship. It can be a written
agreement, or it can be a discussion
bound only by a handshake. Whatever
the form, it should include a
confidentiality requirement, the
duration of the relationship, the
frequency of meetings, the time to be
invested in mentoring activities by
each party, and the specific role of
the mentor.

Development Plan Executed
The protégé and mentor then work
through the development plan as
negotiated in their agreement. This
step is the core of the mentoring
process and continues as long as the
protégé wants to have assistance.

Periodic Meetings
Most mentors and protégés meet for
performance planning, coaching, and
feedback sessions. The frequency of the
meetings depends on the nature of the
relationship. It may also be influenced
by the geographical proximity of the
pair. Some mentoring pairs communicate by telephone more than in face-
to-face meetings.

Reports to Coordinator
When an organization wants to track
and evaluate the results of the
mentoring process, the design may
include periodic reporting to the
coordinator by both the mentor and
the protégé.

Agreement Concludes
A mentoring relationship established to
promote the development of specific
skills or competencies will have a
sunset clause built in. The relationship
may also be concluded when one of the
pair believes it is no longer productive.

for them to work together. It is
important to provide a mechanism for
dissolution without attributing fault to
either person. This is referred to as the
no-fault conclusion.

This model is but one of many effective structures for
facilitating the mentoring relationship. You may have scanned it
thinking that it is a perfect fit for your organization, and you can
use it as a framework for designing your program.

If, however, you want to design your program with additional or different activities, other possibilities are described in
the following sections. Our research has brought a number of
successful mentoring programs with different structures to our
attention. Figures 2 through 7 illustrate six of them in government, accounting, education, and health care. They use a variety
of formats for effective facilitation of the mentoring process. You
may find that one of these programs matches what your organization requires.

Executive Candidate Development Program (ECDP) for the U.S. General Accounting Office

Figure 2 illustrates the mentoring program at the senior-
executive level in a large federal agency, the U.S. General Accounting Office (GAO). The primary objectives of the program
are to:

- Provide the agency with a pool of candidates capable of
  being executives
- Provide the candidates with the knowledge and understanding of the organization necessary for successful
  performance
- Ensure that the executive candidates demonstrate excellence in managerial and technical areas

The Executive Candidate Development Program (ECDP)
has four phases: selection, development, certification, and place-

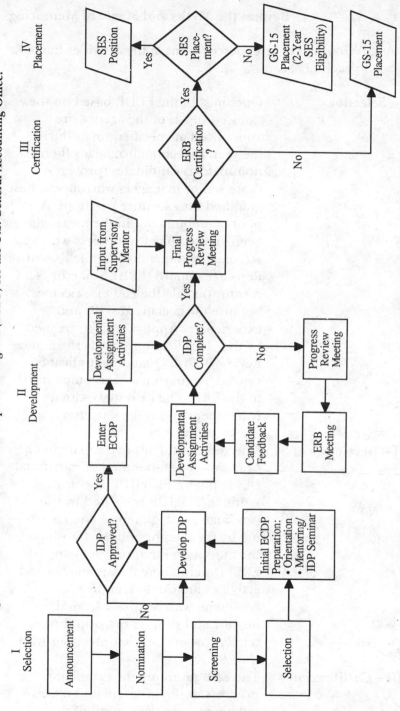

Figure 2. Executive Candidate Development Program (ECDP) for the U.S. General Accounting Office.

Source: Program Coordinator, Executive Candidate Development Program, U.S. General Accounting Office. Used with permission.

ment. Following are brief descriptions of the activities that take place in each phase.

I—Selection	Openings in the ECDP, based on the assessed needs of the agency, are announced at specified times during the year. Division/office heads then nominate as candidates (protégés) those senior managers who appear best qualified for executive positions. A pool of mentors has in the meantime been created from volunteers who were screened and qualified by the Executive Resources Board (ERB). Sometimes a mentor outside the GAO is selected because of specialized skills and experiences. Applicants are screened by the Qualifications and Performance Review Board. Qualified applicants are ranked by quartile and recommended to the ERB. The ERB makes final recommendations for selection into the program.
II—Development	Selected candidates participate in an orientation seminar and an Individual Development Plan (IDP)/mentoring seminar. The IDP is drafted by the candidate, with guidance and counseling by the mentor and the training-institute staff, for approval by the ERB. Developmental assignments and activities are carried out by the candidate with feedback from the mentor and supervisors, and through regular progress-review meetings with the ERB.
III—Certification	The ERB monitors the candidates' progress in the program and makes judgments on certification of the candidates for executive positions.

IV — Placement	The Senior Executive Service (SES) placement decision is made by the ERB with input from supervisors and division/office heads.

Small Public-Sector Mentoring Program

The program in Figure 3 was designed for a small, select group of particularly skilled people in a department of the federal government. In this agency, one job is staffed by specially trained people who develop a high level of expertise during their two- to three-year rotational assignments. Because of the organization's request for confidentiality, the department cannot be named, nor can specific examples that would indicate the nature of the organization be disclosed. But this program is relevant for any organization that needs to groom people for a position requiring special skills. Examples include high-level positions in the financial professions, high-risk jobs such as chemical-plant operator, and service positions such as insurance claims adjusters.

Mentors Identified	In this type of organization, the skilled and experienced job incumbent is the only available mentor, and the only one who can pass on to a new employee the expertise required to perform adequately in the job. Thus, all job incumbents are considered mentors. The option of volunteering is not available.
Mentor Orientation	The orientation is especially important when using this model, as the mentors may not have well-developed interpersonal skills. Their expertise in the technical aspects of the job may be unquestionable, yet they may not have had any opportunity to coach and give feedback. The orientation is designed to include training and practice in these essential skills.

Figure 3. Public-Sector Mentoring Program.

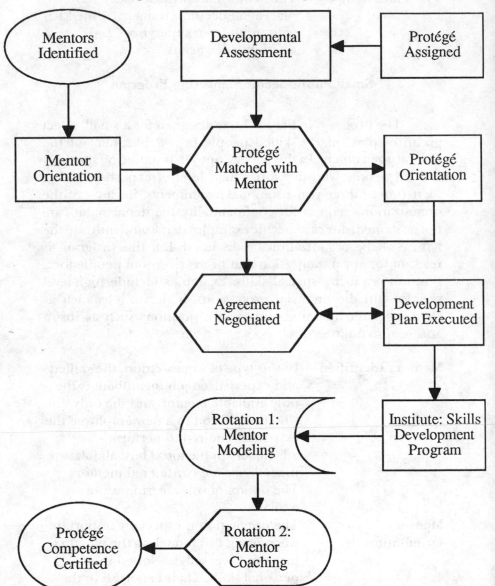

Developmental Needs Assessment	The technical skills needed by protégés in this model are evident and are already specified. Because the organization is training people to do a certain job, it is easy to overlook other developmental needs without systematic assessment of the candidate's strengths and deficiencies. Such an assessment is necessary in order to design and plan a customized development process.
Protégé Matched with Mentor	This step will take place only when there is more than one position to be filled. Because the skills to be learned are already known, the emphasis here is on making the best match of work styles and personalities. It may not be possible to switch mentors if this relationship does not work.
Protégé Orientation	This activity includes all the typical orientation features described in the generic model. Particular stress must be given to timely execution of the development plan because it is likely that the mentor will be leaving the position at a scheduled time and will not be available for further coaching.
Agreement Negotiated	The agreement in this model is particularly important, again because the mentor is likely to be moving on. The meetings and coaching sessions must be firmly fixed.
Development Plan Executed	In this model, there is high risk for the protégé. Often the assignment of the

protégé overlaps that of the mentor for only a short period of time, so the protégé might not have sufficient time to learn the necessary skills. Consequently, any planned developmental activities outside specific job duties may be given secondary priority by both the mentor and the protégé.

Protégé Institute   The design includes a dedicated time of formal training for the protégé at a training institute. The content of such training may be both job-specific and generic. As part of it, the mentor may be involved with coaching the protégé on individual study activities.

Mentor Modeling   An initial period of time is set aside for the mentor to model or demonstrate all the skills and competencies to be learned by the protégé. The protégé is an observer and learner during this phase.

Mentor Coaching   During this part of the process, the protégé takes the active role with the mentor acting as coach. In a high-risk situation, the potential hazard is mitigated by having the experienced person available as the protégé builds confidence.

Protégé Competence Certified   The mentoring relationship concludes when the competence of the protégé is certified, or when a decision is reached not to certify the protégé for the position. It may also conclude when the transfer or departure date for the mentor is reached. In such cases, protégés may be able to be matched with other mentors to continue the training.

Mentoring Program for a Small Accounting Firm

Figure 4 illustrates a program designed for a small accounting firm, Rooney, Ida, Nolt and Ahern, headquartered in Oakland, California. This program was born when the firm recognized the staff's need for guidance and support in achieving personal and professional goals. The program goals include:

- Communicating firm policies and expectations to staff
- Assisting staff in identifying opportunities for growth and specialization offered within the firm
- Assisting staff in setting, monitoring, and achieving congruent personal and firm goals
- Assisting staff in career-development decisions
- Responsively addressing problems encountered by staff
- Increasing job satisfaction
- Assisting in developing staff
- Encouraging sharing of experiences and use of talents among all members of the firm

The program is available to every one of the 100 employees on a voluntary basis and is administered by the personnel manager. Because staff members have short-term serial assignments with managers who are in charge of an audit or tax review, the firm wanted a process that would add a consistent focus on individual development activities. The mentoring program was implemented to meet this need. The identification of mentors and protégés, called *participants* in this program, proceeds simultaneously. Most of the components of the generic model are applied in this program. The descriptions here cite specific differences from that model.

**Figure 4. Mentoring Program Activity Flow for Rooney, Ida, Nolt
and Ahern, Certified Public Accountants.**

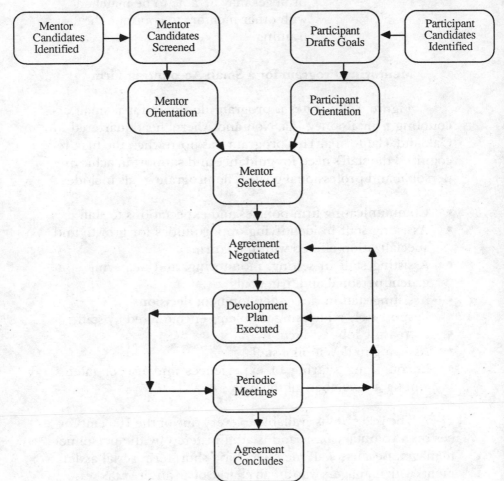

Source: Graphic designed from Rooney, Ida, Nolt and Ahern, Certified Public Accountants, mentoring program description. Used with permission.

Mentor Candidates Identified

The goal is to have an adequate pool of mentors to make appropriate matches with participants on a timely basis. Mentors volunteer to participate, sometimes at the suggestion of the managing partner or other senior staff. Volunteering indicates interest in the program and willingness to function as a mentor.

A call for volunteers is extended two times each year, and anyone may volunteer at other times. For example, if the firm hires a manager with particular expertise in management information systems, this person could quickly be matched with another member of the firm for mentoring and coaching on information systems.

Mentor Candidates Screened

The personnel manager receives the names of five mentor candidates from each person who wants to become a participant (protégé). Essentially, the participants are screening the mentors, as the program's goal is to match participants with their first or second choice. The presumption is that the nominated mentors have the skills and abilities wanted by the participants.

Mentor Orientation

This program had one large orientation for mentors and participants in the beginning. The mission, goals, and projected growth of the firm were described, as well as how the mentoring program supports the mission and goals. Policies and procedures relevant to promotion were part of the orientation, as was the availability of educational and developmental resources. The orientation included details of the mentoring program— development plans, types of agreements that might be negotiated— recognition for mentors, and a description of the coordinator's role.

Individual orientations to the program take place when a new employee joins the firm. At that time, all these subjects are discussed, and the individual has the opportunity to express interest in the program.

Participant Candidates Identified

As stated, the program is open to any employee. Typical characteristics and responsibilities of the participants, such as willingness to assume responsibility for one's own growth and development, are published in the personnel manual.

Participant Drafts Goals

Participants are expected to draft a statement of developmental needs, set goals, and formulate an action plan for discussion with the mentor.

Participant Orientation

As stated, the initial orientation was a group session for both mentors and participants. As new people join the firm, they learn about the mentoring program in the basic orientation for new staff members.

Mentor Selected

The goal is to match every participant with his or her first or second choice of mentor. A matrix of the mentor/ participant relationships is maintained by the coordinator, who works with department heads and other leaders of the firm to determine the most appropriate matches.

Agreement Negotiated	An outline of the subjects to be included in the agreement is provided to all interested participants and mentors. Some pairs elect not to use the suggested format as a record of the agreement, although most use it as a guide for the discussion.
Development Plan Executed	During the course of the relationship, the participant is expected to maintain documentation on developmental goals, action plans, and accomplishments. Regular contact with the coordinator is a part of the plan and the responsibility of each participant.
Periodic Meetings	The mentor/participant pairs are expected to meet regularly for planning activities, coaching, and feedback. The firm picks up the tab for lunch for some of these meetings. In addition, the coordinator chairs periodic meetings with mentors and participants.
Agreement Concludes	The relationship can be concluded at the agreed time or when either party can no longer meet the specified obligations. It may also end ahead of the established time if the participant attains all goals set with the current mentor and wants to develop different skills or knowledge with another mentor.

College Mentoring Program to Introduce Students to Work World

Figure 5 represents the Trinity College Mentoring Program in Washington, D.C. The primary goal of the program is to offer selected student mentees (protégés) the opportunity to work with a mentor in a professional area related to her academic major or career interests. Additional outcomes are:

- Providing a professional role model for students
- Students have a view of work in a profession
- Students have access to someone who has been through college, job, and family transitions
- Mentors give something back to Trinity
- Alumnae keep up with Trinity and its students
- Alumnae give ongoing attention to their own careers
- Mentor program presents the college as one that works

The program differs from an internship in that work skills or experience need not be the primary focus. Mentors are expected to provide support, encouragement, and important perspectives on issues that women face in today's professional world. It is also hoped that lasting career networks and friendships will result.

Two important components help manage and structure this program. The director coordinates the day-to-day aspects, such as contacting mentors and students, and managing the database and mentor/mentee orientations. The Mentor Program Committee, which is made up of faculty and the current executive director of the Alumni Association, acts in an advisory capacity to the director. For example, the committee members usually know the mentee candidates and mentors quite well. This personal knowledge helps in the mentor/mentee screening and matching process. The committee also advises on problem resolution and program changes.

Committee Chair Mary Hayes (interview by author, 1990) reports that the program is a great success and will be a permanent service of the college. Both potential mentors and student protégés are overwhelmingly interested in keeping the program going. Here is how it works.

Mentor Candidates Identified   A letter and questionnaire are sent out jointly by the Trinity Career and

Figure 5. Trinity College Mentoring Program.

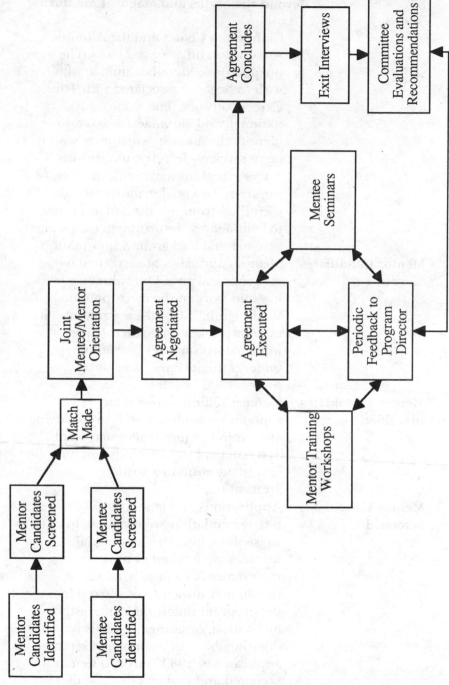

Source: Graphic designed from Trinity College program description. Used with permission.

Counseling Center and the Alumni Association on a regular basis. The purpose is to identify alumnae who wish to become associated with Trinity's Career Network. The database is national, and alumnae are asked to identify the areas in which they wish to be of service—lectures, internships, career panel presentations, the mentor program. Potential mentors are initially identified from this list and are asked to volunteer by returning personal and professional background information.

Mentor Candidates Screened   Mentor candidates are screened by geographical area. Only alumnae who live and work in the metropolitan Washington, D.C., area are put into the mentor pool. A database includes information such as class; employer; undergraduate, graduate, and professional degrees.

Mentee Candidates Identified   Mentees self-nominate yearly. Any sophomore student who is not studying abroad in her junior year may apply. Two letters of recommendation must be sent in addition to a written application.

Mentee Candidates Screened   Applications and letters of recommendation are reviewed. In subsequent interviews, potential mentees are advised of program requirements. Generally, all self-nominated students are allowed into the program unless their interest, motivation, or academic status is questionable. For example, of seventeen applicants in 1989, only two were not accepted and that was because they missed interviews.

Match Made	The Mentor Program Committee usually matches mentor and mentee on the basis of the self-diagnosed professional needs of the mentee. If the mentee states an interest in a marketing career, she will likely be matched with a former business major or a marketing professional.
Joint Mentee/ Mentor Orientation	The mentor and mentee meet at a group reception or orientation. During this gathering, presentations are made about program expectations.
Agreement Negotiated	The mentor and mentee decide on the types of activities they will work on together. The director makes general suggestions, but the actual agreement is set by only the two parties.
Mentor Training Workshops	During the course of the relationship, mentors attend one formal workshop and at least one informal social event, which cover role orientation, expectations, and training. Mentors share their experiences and discuss relationship issues.
Mentee Seminars	Mentees attend three seminars each semester that focus on career-related issues. They also do personal assessments and participate in assertiveness training.
Periodic Feedback to Program Director	The director keeps in constant contact with the mentor and student to monitor the relationship. If problems surface, the director may ask the Mentor Program Committee for procedural advice.
Agreement Concludes	The relationship continues for three semesters and ends with the conclusion of the mentee's first senior semester.

Exit Interviews   Mentees are interviewed by two
                             committee members to gather data
                             about the program and their mentor's
                             performance.

Committee   The Mentor Program Committee
Evaluations and   evaluates the interviews and
Recommendations   recommends any policy or procedural
                             changes to the director.

Mentoring Program in Health Care

Figure 6 is a model for a mentor program in the field of
health care. It pairs new or inexperienced tumor registrars with
experienced ones. The mentor program is run by the Tumor
Registrars Association of California (TRAC), a joint professional
and volunteer organization. Tumor registrars have the primary
responsibilities of identifying, registering, and reporting cancer
cases. They record demographic data and also information on
type of cancer, stage of the disease, and treatment. The registrars
follow up these cases yearly to record the progress of treatment.
Tumor registrars must have a basic knowledge of anatomy and
physiology along with skills in data collection and analysis of
cancer data, and knowledge of cancer management.

A 1985 State of California law requires that health care
professionals and organizations report all cancer cases to the
Department of Health Services. This information is used by the
state to track incidents of cancer, causes, and survival rates.
Since the mandatory law was passed, the need for experienced
tumor registrars has increased. The TRAC program was developed to increase the skills and confidence of new tumor registrars by allowing them to network and consult with experienced
role models who provide guidance and serve as resources. The
basic program goal is to augment the formal education of protégés, which is a two-year college curriculum, or their formal
training in basic registry skills. Other objectives are to help
protégés

• Meet state certification requirements
• Increase the level of productivity in tumor registries

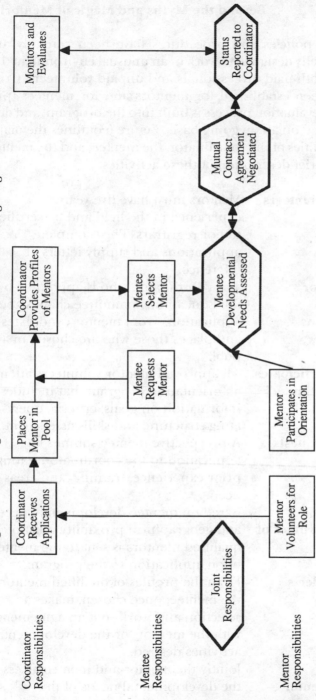

Figure 6. Tumor Registrars Association of California Mentoring Program.

Source: Graphic designed from Tumor Registrars Association of California mentoring program description. Used with permission.

The policies and procedures have been carefully and professionally designed to work in an unusual environment that includes both paid professionals and unpaid volunteers. Criteria have been established for mentors and for mentees (protégés). An evaluation process is built into the program, and data are collected on an on-going basis. Figure 6 outlines the major responsibilities of the coordinator, the mentee, and the mentor. Here is a brief description of these activities:

Mentor Volunteers for Role	Mentors must have five years experience in the field and be certified tumor registrars. They complete applications and supply letters of reference.
Coordinator Receives Applications	The coordinator, who is appointed by the Education Committee chair, screens applications from mentor candidates and places those who are chosen in a pool.
Mentor Participates in Orientation	All approved mentor volunteers attend an orientation program that includes information on goals, criteria, operating structure, and skills assessment.
Mentee Requests Mentor	A prospective mentee submits an application to the coordinator, stating prior experience, training, and areas of need.
Coordinator Provides Profiles of Mentors	Based on mentee developmental needs and geographical proximity, a list of qualified mentors is sent to the mentee upon application to the program.
Mentee Selects Mentor	From the profiles of qualified mentors, the mentee, once chosen, makes a selection and works out an agreement with the mentor for the developmental activities desired.
Mentee Developmental Needs Assessed	Jointly the mentor and mentee assess the developmental needs of the mentee.

Mutual Contract Agreement Negotiated	After verbal acceptance, a written contract specifying the services to be provided is signed by both parties.
Status Reported to Coordinator	Quarterly reports are made to the coordinator by both the mentor and the mentee. A final report is sent at termination of the agreement.
Monitors and Evaluates	The coordinator monitors all operations of the program through review of applications, telephone contact with mentors and mentees, review of contracts, and status reports. Mentors are evaluated yearly, and the entire program is evaluated by the Education Committee.

College Mentoring Program at Empire State College

Since its founding in 1971 Empire State College of the State University of New York (SUNY-ESC) has employed mentoring for academic advisement and instruction. The college maintains a core faculty at seven major centers throughout New York State. Faculty mentors at SUNY-ESC, representing many arts and sciences disciplines, assist students, who are professionals and working adults, in developing personalized degree programs. The term *mentor* adopted by the faculty is not only a conscious variation within the teaching profession but its rich variations also mirror the roles that mentors play outside of higher education in companies and organizations (H. Hammett, interview by author, 1989). Mentors and students (protégés) employ learning contracts to create guided, individualized studies. This flexible mentoring program, illustrated in Figure 7, has these objectives:

- Adult students will design rigorous and relevant learning programs with mentors.
- Students will have control over the pacing of college studies, enabling them to balance job, home, and school obligations.
- Learning at work will be linked with formal college studies.

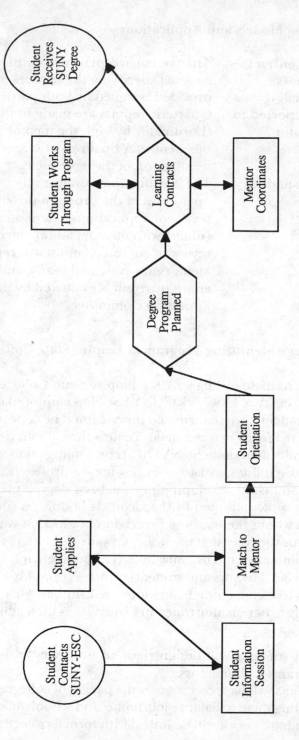

Figure 7. Empire State College Mentoring Program.

Source: Graphic designed from Empire State College mentoring program description. Used with permission.

The components of the mentoring process at Empire are:

Student Contacts SUNY-ESC	A potential student contacts the college.
Student Information Session	Potential students attend an information session and receive an application and financial-aid materials.
Student Applies	Application is received and accepted by the college, and student is invited to an orientation.
Match to Mentor	An associate dean reviews the student's application and the mentor data and makes a match with a primary mentor.
Student Orientation	Student then attends orientation, meets the primary mentor, and enrolls in the program.
Degree Program Planned	Student and mentor assess prior learning and plan a degree program.
Learning Contracts	Student and mentor then negotiate a series of learning contracts. All contracts are reviewed by the dean or associate dean (N. Hanawi, interview with author, 1989).
Student Works Through Program	Student works through the learning activities with the primary mentor and other faculty mentors.
Mentor Coordinates	Throughout the progression of learning contracts, the mentors serve as guides, coaches, and advisers, and suggest other learning experiences.
Evaluation	Both the primary mentor and the student write a narrative evaluation of what the student has learned in the process.

In the beginning of this chapter, Figure 1 described a

model for a facilitated mentoring program; that model contains all the components that research and experience suggest a successful program should have. In the following chapters you will find detailed guidelines for designing and implementing the processes described.

7

Assessing Needs
and Determining
Organizational Readiness

This chapter assumes that you believe facilitated mentoring is a good, workable way to develop people. Now you have to decide whether it will work in your organization. To make that decision, you must, first, establish whether your organization needs a mentoring program, and, second, determine whether the culture of your organization will support such a program. As the experiences related in previous chapters show, successful facilitated mentoring programs require careful planning, commitment, and support. The steps outlined in this chapter will help you determine your organization's readiness for such a program.

Determine Your Organization's Future
Succession Planning Needs

Are there any data to justify a mentoring program in your organization? Does your organization really have that need? One way to answer these questions is take a good look at your future personnel needs through succession planning. Succession planning is more than projecting your future human-resource requirements. It also means designing strategies for getting people who are in the organization ready to fill those requirements.

When you do succession planning, keep in mind that all the data you are analyzing are about the past. What you have always been doing may not be a relevant approach in today's volatile environment. Try to avoid being constrained by past history, no matter how good the results were or how comfortable the old, familiar ways of doing things are. Because succession planning is about the future, you will require more than historical data to make the most useful projections for your organization.

Good succession planning also involves looking both at your organization and at the larger environment in which it operates. What factors nearby and around the globe will have an impact on your organization's goals? Trends, especially the coming labor shortage and the increasingly cross-cultural nature of the work force, must be considered. In her "State of the Workforce" address (1990) Elizabeth Dole, Secretary of Labor, expressed the potential need in this way: "The skills of a large number of experienced workers are now obsolete or soon will be made obsolete by changes in technology. . . . There is no doubt that our work force crisis is a challenge to education, labor, business, and government." Are you expecting significant technological changes in your industry or in the equipment you use? Technological changes can create a demand for new skills, unusual knowledge, and different attitudes.

Is your company a target for a takeover or merger? What will changes in world-trade agreements do to the demand for your product or service? Obviously you will not be analyzing each of these indicators in depth in preparation for designing a mentoring program. We mention these external factors at this point to prompt you to consider the broad spectrum of challenges in creating an organization that can get results today and tomorrow. Succession planning is, in the end, creating plans to perpetuate your organization.

This is not meant to be an exhaustive list of the issues and concerns of your organization today, but it can trigger you to think of specific impacts you may anticipate. Not even the most skillful and knowledgeable planners can anticipate all the possible variables. The best that can be done is to gather the most accurate data available, write down the assumptions that are made about both the data and the future, and then make plans using the combined judgment of a planning team.

You can use several methods to assess the number and type of employees your organization will need. Prange and Smalley (1988) outline several techniques for making work-force projections that are practical even for small organizations. They caution that each of the techniques is a different way of thinking about the future and each will yield a different projection. The four techniques they describe are:

- Trend extrapolation
- Delphi probes
- Scenarios
- Precursor

Trend extrapolation plots past data with discovered curves extrapolated into the future. This technique is applicable for estimating attrition from the aging and retirement of employees.

Delphi probes are polls of experts done several times to obtain a consensus of intuitive estimates of the future. Such combined guesses can prove valuable, or they can be an accumulation of ignorance. Those selected for their intuition about future employment factors might be economists, demographic researchers, international business and commerce experts, and futurists.

Scenarios involve writing a story about or description of the future, usually telling how to get there from here. Visioning or speculation of this type may be appropriate when you anticipate that your organization will be strongly affected by technological or social change.

Precursor forecasting assumes a correlation between events in various environments. For example, an economic downturn has a negative impact on sales of big-ticket or gift items such as luxury automobiles. The manufacturers of these products and suppliers of raw materials for them can then expect a slowing demand in their own industry. By looking at these precursors, the manufacturers of necessity goods, such as clothing, food, and building materials, can also predict the timing of slowdowns in their industries.

You can use one or a combination of techniques to get the greatest precision in your estimate of people needs for the next five or ten years. Keep in mind when projecting human-resource requirements that you are looking for more than numbers. You also want to know what kinds of skills your employees must have to do the jobs.

The next question to answer in succession planning is, Where will we get these employees? Do your projections for movement of current employees indicate that an adequate number are ready to be promoted to supervisory and management positions? Are current recruitment and hiring practices producing the required numbers of people with the types of skills desired? And finally, will current practices allow the organization to meet its goals for promoting minorities and women? If the answers to these three questions are no or maybe, you have some justification for a structured mentoring program. If your preliminary decision about mentoring is a go, continue your readiness assessment by taking a close look inside the organization at the beliefs and values of the managers.

Examine the Organization's Commitment to Human Resource Development

The acid test of a commitment to the development of people is whether upper-level managers would rather grow competence than buy it. Such an indication of top-management support is critical to the success and continuity of a mentoring program. When executive management believes that development programs make a difference, such programs will be given a high priority by all members of the organization. You probably already have some feeling for your organization's commitment to human resource development. The last time you were scheduled to attend a training workshop or seminar out of town and a crisis occurred at work, did your boss say, "Sorry, but we need you here"? Or was the message "That training is important; we can handle things here"?

A mentoring program will not typically have such visible costs as the registration fees for an outside workshop. However, allowing the mentor and protégé to meet and engage in important coaching and feedback discussions may mean a loss of productive time. If a commitment to allowing time to be used for development activities is not already firmly entrenched in the organization, facilitated mentoring is probably not a good idea.

Determine the Scope of the Mentoring Program

The next factor to assess is the scope of the proposed mentoring program. Does the need for developing people extend across all functions and down through all levels? Will this be a long-term need? Or is there a temporary need to facilitate the development of a special target group such as women or people of particular ethnicity in order to meet affirmative-action goals and timetables?

Most experienced users of mentoring programs advise to start small and expand after a period of successful operation. This tactic will give you a program of manageable size while you accumulate experience and work out the kinks in your policies and operating procedures.

Similarly, those who have experience setting up mentoring programs advise that the duration of the formal relationship between the mentor and protégé be on the brief side at first. "Begin with a short program—six months is long enough for specified learning to occur without making the commitment too burdensome" (Phillips-Jones, 1983). Again, this trial period can be used to get feedback, work out problems, and keep motivated mentors and protégés from repeated discouraging experiences.

Assess the Organization's Ability to Sustain the Characteristics of Successful Mentoring Programs

The continuing study of mentoring programs has revealed some characteristics that are essential for their success. A quick way to assess your organization's readiness for a formal, structured mentoring program is to determine the degree to which each of the following characteristics can be successfully sustained in your environment.

Voluntary Participation. Almost everyone with firsthand experience in a mentoring program, and many who have researched them and written about them, stresses voluntary participation by both mentor and protégé. The necessary enthusiasm and commitment will not occur when mentors and protégés are drafted. On an individual level, the recommendation is that people be invited to become involved and not be forced to do so if they are reluctant to participate.

➤   *Look for volunteers, not draftees.*

Skipped-Level Mentors. Does your organization have sufficient numbers of people to match protégés with mentors who are two or more levels higher? This distance will minimize the concern of the mentor that the protégé is out to get his or her job. A protégé who is at the next level below can be a too-close-for-comfort competitor to the mentor.

➤   *Identify a pool of mentors at the highest possible levels.*

Cross-Functional Pairing. It is sometimes complicated to administer pairing across functional lines in an organization, but the benefits are many. The mentor from another department brings broad experiences that will enhance the learning of the protégé. Also, when the protégé has targeted a future position in a different department or function, it is advantageous to select a mentor from that area. Knowledge of the skills required for jobs in the target area will be relevant for the protégé. In addition, the communication and political network in the new department can be readily accessed with the help of a mentor who has been working there. The ideal mentor will also have had experience in the protégé's current department or function.

➤   *Look for mentor candidates across functions.*

Flexible Duration. The initial duration of the relationship in most programs is six months to two years. Anything much longer or shorter is probably not cost-effective or practical to administer. Whatever the agreed time period, it must be long enough to meet the needs of the protégé and short enough to coincide with the availability of the mentor. The protégé who wants exposure to a department will need less time than one who wants to work on a long-term project with a mentor's help. Thus, the time period should be adjustable within set parameters based on the protégé's goals.

➤ *Set a flexible conclusion date that meets the protégé's needs.*

One-on-One Mentoring. This recommendation, like all the others, must be kept flexible. Many competent and experienced mentors function in two or more relationships all the time. But in the beginning it is wise to keep the mentoring on a one-to-one basis until the novice mentor has a chance to gauge how much time will be spent in the role.

➤ *Keep the mentor with one protégé until experience, competence, and willingness allow for more.*

No-Fault Conclusion. When the mentoring relationship doesn't jell or if it turns sour for either party, there must be a way to conclude it without damage to anyone. This feature must be a part of the policy and procedure and should be emphasized during the orientation and agreement negotiations.

➤ *Establish and emphasize the no-fault conclusion at the beginning of the program.*

Integration with Total Development Effort. When the mentoring program is a separate, special program, the responsibilities for it and for other human-resource-development activities tend to become cloudy. Separate programs are also vulnerable to budget cuts. When mentoring is seen as one module of a comprehensive development process, it can be readily integrated with the career-planning, training, and other development activities already offered in the organization. In an adult-education organization (Appel and Trail, 1986), among the essential conditions cited as favorable for mentoring are (1) administrative support for continued learning; (2) a budget commitment to support staff development; (3) policies and procedures for planning, implementing, and evaluating; (4) a staffing pattern to ensure that staff is fully informed and involved in major program decisions; and (5) recognition of the significance of orientation, in-service education, other professional development opportunities, and mentoring as major interrelated components of a total program of staff development.

➤   *Look for ways to integrate mentoring into existing human resource development programs.*

   High Priority for Evaluation. Top management must support continued evaluation of the program. The evaluation format and strategies should be designed at the beginning in order to collect uncontaminated data for comparison. To start the process, a database of current results in recruiting, hiring, training, and promoting people throughout the organization must be established. Chapter Thirteen outlines the possible types of data you might want. Tracking the results of mentoring processes can be done through periodic reports from mentors, protégés, and natural bosses, through interviews, through analysis of promotions, and in other ways.
   Evaluation does two things. Most obviously, it provides important information on how well the program is working. More importantly, it can be an important tool in getting organizational members to buy into the program. For example, operational managers tend to abdicate responsibility for the development of their people because they have been led to believe training is the role of the training department or a similar function in human resources. In order to emphasize the manager's responsibility for training and developing subordinates,

the mentoring coordinator must insist that the boss be an active participant in development planning and in negotiating the agreement with the mentor, and also in assessing how well that plan worked. When changes are made as a result of the boss's feedback, support will grow for the program.

➤   *Give mentoring program evaluation a high priority.*

Creation and Communication of Policies and Procedures. A task force or program advisory board may be established to work out policies and procedures. This approach is particularly valuable when the program is to be available to anyone in the organization and when it is likely there will be cross-functional pairs. An advisory board of high-level managers or administrators who represent each of the functional areas can collaborate on a design to maximize the benefits and minimize the risks.

➤   *Create and communicate clear policy and procedures.*

Promotional Campaign. It is important that the organization promote the program. The promotion can be both informative and motivational. The information must include the criteria for participation, the policy for engaging in development activities on company time, what (if any) guarantees are included for successful protégés, how the mentors will be rewarded, and how to get out of a bad situation. In addition, promotion can create enthusiasm for involvement. Building a positive image of the mentoring program will stimulate support and participation by mentors, protégés, bosses, and others.

➤   *Plan the promotion to sell the program and processes.*

Checklist

When you glance back at this list of important considerations, you can see that establishing a structured mentoring program is a serious commitment. Exhibit 1 asks important questions that will help you to determine your organization's readiness for facilitated mentoring. On the checklist, write the actions you can take to get the information you need to make this important decision. Obviously you will have identified other factors that will influence the readiness of your organization. Add those items to the checklist so you have a complete action plan when you finish.

Exhibit 1. Checklist for Determining Organizational Readiness.

	Action to Take
1. What personnel needs do we have that would justify starting a facilitated mentoring program?	
2. Are top-level executives prepared to commit time and money to human resource development? In what visible ways will they make this commitment?	
3. What is the scope of the proposed pilot program in terms of: —target group? —functional areas? —levels? —duration? —size? —duration of each relationship?	
4. Will voluntary participation work here?	
5. Are there sufficient numbers of skipped-level mentors?	
6. Is cross-functional pairing desirable? How will we administer it?	
7. Can the duration of the program be flexible?	
8. Will a no-fault conclusion be acceptable?	
9. How will facilitated mentoring fit with other human resource development programs?	

Exhibit 1. Checklist for Determining Organizational Readiness, Cont'd.

---

10. Will one-on-one mentoring be possible?   _____
                                                          _____

11. Will evaluation be given high priority?   _____
                                                          _____

12. Who will establish policies and procedures?   _____
                                                          _____

13. What are the available promotional vehicles?   _____
                                                          _____

14. _____   _____
    _____   _____

15. _____   _____
    _____   _____

8

Structuring the Mentor Role: Qualifications, Recruitment, Selection, and Rewards

The mentor role deserves your most careful attention as it is the linchpin in the mentoring relationship and in the facilitated program. Competence and commitment are the unequivocal characteristics of a successful mentor. Qualifying candidates for the mentor role must build from the foundation of being willing and able to help another person to grow. The types of capabilities and the nature of the commitment will vary with each mentor/protégé relationship.

Having read this far in the book, you probably have some good ideas about using mentors in your development programs. You have also, no doubt, already thought of the many obstacles you may face in implementing your mentoring program. In this chapter you will find specific guidelines for defining the role of the mentor, for recruiting mentors, for creating the mechanisms for establishing a pool of qualified mentors, and for making the mentoring role work well.

For every guideline suggested here you can probably find an exception in a mentoring program somewhere. For example, I have talked with people who have had successful peer mentoring relationships and with people whose mentors were younger than themselves. Likewise, there are many examples of bosses who function as mentors to some of their subordinates. That is fine. Perhaps the only unbreakable rule about facilitated mentoring is that the program be designed for maximum flexibility and fulfill the needs of the organization. For clarity and ease of description, the processes described in this chapter will follow the generic facilitated mentoring model presented in Chapter Six.

Qualifications

An individual may be a superb role model, do all of the things a sponsor does, yet not have the skills to perform effectively as a mentor. Several specific skills and attributes necessary to carry out the functions of a mentor have emerged from our experience with the design, implementation, and evaluation of mentoring programs for management-level people. These hallmarks of master mentors (Everitt and Murray-Hicks, 1981) are:

- Strong interpersonal skills
- Organizational knowledge
- Exemplary supervisory skills
- Technical competence
- Personal power and charisma
- Status and prestige
- Willingness to be responsible for someone else's growth
- Ability to share credit
- Patience and risk taking

Use the following brief descriptions of the characteristics to help you to recognize the most likely mentor candidates in your organization. Each description is followed by the key element to look for.

Strong Interpersonal Skills. Mentors enjoy being with people; they like interacting with others. The potential mentor is the animated talker in the middle of a group, not the solitary figure off on the sidelines engrossed in a newspaper. Because the mentor role demands close relationships, the best candidate is one who enjoys working with people more than working alone or working with things.

Of course there are always exceptions. An individual may be unusually skillful in a professional or technical area—for example, research methodology—and not have good communication skills. A persistent protégé may be able to extract the desired assistance from such a person. But beware of pairing a passive protégé with a strong, silent type as mentor. One of the two must be capable and willing to initiate contact and work at keeping the relationship going.

➤   *Look for a person who both talks and listens.*

Knowledge of the Organization. The most helpful mentor is one who has intimate knowledge of the vision and long-range goals of the organization. To access this information, the mentor must have an open line to both the formal and informal communication channels within the organization.

Having a mentor who is able to tap into an extensive network of movers and shakers can significantly expand the resources available to the protégé. Knowing where the organization is going (and how quickly or slowly) enables the mentor to assess the reality of the protégé's aspirations. The mentor will know where the opportunities are based on projected growth, direction, and goals of the organization. If the organization is downsizing, the mentor can direct the protégé into appropriate areas, such as a lateral move into a different function.

➤   *Look for a person with an extensive network of resources.*

Exemplary Supervisory Skills. The following management skills seem to be essential for competent performance as a mentor:

- Planning performance—helping others to set objectives, create action plans, estimate resource requirements, schedule time
- Appraising performance—observing another's performance, evaluating it, and determining the appropriate type of feedback
- Giving feedback and coaching—providing feedback that

clearly reinforces desired performance or coaches to improve performance to agreed standards

- Modeling—demonstrating desirable techniques for task performance
- Delegating—determining appropriate tasks to be delegated to a person capable of performing those tasks; negotiating agreement on the tasks to be performed, time for completion, authorities to be consulted, and resources to be used

The list could go on. However, these are the basics, the survival skills for supervisors.

At this point you might be thinking, Why are these skills especially important in a mentor? Everyone who supervises should have these skills! Of course they should. However, many people are promoted to supervisory positions because they are the best workers. In all fields—craft, technical, and professional—many people without supervisory experience or skills are assigned to jobs that require overseeing the work of subordinates. Rarely is a person's leadership potential assessed in any systematic way before promotional decisions are made. Furthermore, few people are prepared or trained for the supervisory role. The misconception is that if they can do the work, they can also get it done through others. According to one researcher (Davis, 1981, p. 10), "Mentoring/coaching requires very good interpersonal skills such as communication [particularly questioning and listening], motivating, encouraging, delegating, and so forth. These skills are most likely the least developed for a middle or upper manager." This situation is not likely to change in the near future, so it is important to carefully screen mentor candidates for basic supervisory competence. It is not enough to want to be a mentor. One has to have the proven skills.

➤ *Look for a person who has managed groups of people successfully or who has chaired committees and task forces.*

Technical Competence. It may seem obvious that the mentor should be competent in the skill area the protégé wants to develop. However, certain organizations have set up mentoring programs and made matches on the basis of the mentor's position and the protégé's membership in a target group. Little or no thought is given to the skill deficiencies of the protégé and none to the relevant competence of the mentor.

Ideally, the mentor will be skilled and experienced in two or more functions of the organization. The mentor who draws from a broad background can offer a variety of examples and a deep, rich experience to the protégé. In addition, the mentor with extensive experience is less likely to see the protégé as an immediate rival for promotions or other perks.

➤ *Look for a person who has skills the protégé needs plus skills in at least one other technical or professional area.*

Status and Prestige. Status of the mentor may be unimportant when the relationship is invisible to others. But when a program is public and designed to groom people for increased responsibility, the mentors must have prestige and know how to share it with their protégés.

Why should mentors be prestigious? First, only a high-status mentor will know the organization well enough to guide someone else. Second, a basic principle of behavior modeling is that people are likely to emulate someone who is perceived as having prestige. Few people consciously imitate the actions of a person regarded as a bad example. The development process will be easier and more efficient when the mentor is held in high esteem than when he or she is not.

➤ *Find the person who makes the news and is respected.*

Personal Power. Positive regard and respect for others in the organization makes the mentor a powerful magnet of leadership. Sometimes this quality is called charisma. It is easy to recognize those who have it and those who do not. People are quickly attracted to the charismatic leader. It may be part of that mysterious attraction that is often cited as the genesis of informal mentoring relationships. Although the manifestations of personal power may be learned behaviors, these are not skills that can be readily taught.

➤ *Look for the person whose opinions are sought.*

Willingness to Be Responsible for Someone Else's Growth. You cannot draft people to be mentors. The tangible and intangible rewards of helping someone else to grow make some people willing and eager to accept such an awesome responsibility. Some managers share my opinion that people are ultimately responsible for their own growth and development; however, the policies and practices of many organizations have taught people that they cannot be responsible for themselves. Self-management is discouraged when employees are told what to do and when to do it, what to learn and when to learn it. It will take many years for traditionally managed organizations to change this system and encourage self-responsibility for growth and development. As an interim step, responsibility for development can be shared by the organization, the individual's boss, the mentor, and the individual.

A mentor who is secure about his or her own competence is likely to be generous with time spent in helping others to grow. It may be an added incentive to remind mentor candidates that it adds to their credentials to be seen as a star maker.

➤ *Look for a person who initiates coaching contacts with others.*

Ability to Share Credit. The exceptional mentor demonstrates that there is sufficient credit and recognition for everyone to share. This superstar can step out of the limelight and let the protégé take the bows. Good mentors will neither claim the protégé's work as their own nor attribute their own work to the protégé.

➤ *Look for a person who talks and behaves teamwork.*

Patience in Risky Situations. This attribute may be the most important—and the least measurable—of all. Having the patience and courage to let a protégé risk and fail, all the while being there to provide support, takes unusual fortitude. Perhaps the most important function mentors have is creating the opportunities for protégés to prove themselves in risky situations (Collins and Scott, 1978). But they must also be prudent about those risks and let protégés develop at their own speed. There is a fine line between knowing when to allow a protégé to muddle through and knowing when to provide help. Mentors who jump in too quickly may be pushing their protégés' development.

> ➤ *Look for a person who says, "Give it a try!"*

It may seem impossible to find all these qualifications in the mentors you are seeking. The best suggestion is to get as much as you can, and expect to help the mentors develop additional skills as they work with the protégés.

Recruitment Strategies

In any discussion of facilitated programs, the first thing people ask about is the source of mentors. Where will they come from? Who will be willing to give the necessary time and energy to work diligently to help someone else to grow? Important reputations and large egos will be on the line. What if things don't work out? What if those who do accept give only lip service to the role without spending quality time with the protégés? Sometimes these questions are not asked aloud, but the issues lurk as potential obstacles to the success of the program.

The people who complain about the dearth of mentors may be looking in the wrong places and at the wrong people. Look around you, not just at the highest levels. To find people throughout the organization, who are willing to help others by mentoring, consider the following recruiting strategies.

Using Volunteers. Using volunteering as a strategy for recruitment entails having clearly stated criteria. Fortunately, most people know whether they enjoy instructing and coaching. But not everyone possesses the ability to make an objective assessment of his or her own readiness to carry out all the

Exhibit 2. Sample Call for Volunteer Mentors.

Desirable Characteristics of Mentors

Everyone is encouraged to develop the skills and competencies to function effectively as a mentor. Mentors are asked to volunteer for the *mentor pool*. Mentors are expected to have most of the following characteristics:

- Willingness to assume and visibly demonstrate leadership
- People oriented behavior
- Regarded as successful in the Firm
- Willingness to assume responsibility and accountability as a mentor
- Knowledgeable about the Firm's goals, policies, functions, communication channels, training programs, etc.
- Willingness to help set development goals, coach, and give feedback
- Aware of resources available within and outside the Firm
- Committed to the development of staff
- Willingness to share personal experiences relevant to the needs of the participant

---

Source: Adapted from Everitt and Murray-Hicks, 1981.

necessary mentoring responsibilities. Use the qualifications described previously in this chapter to develop a list of criteria for your mentor candidates. Add to the list any specific technical or professional skills you will require. Exhibit 2 is a sample call for volunteers.

Using Nomination by Executives. Another option for recruiting mentors is to have top management and administrative people nominate candidates for the mentor pool. Nominators should use prestated criteria when considering and selecting these nominees. At Rooney, Ida, Nolt and Ahern, a small accounting firm where every high-level person is well-known to the others, the managing partner, senior partners, and department heads are asked to provide an initial list of nominees for the mentor pool. The coordinator, who is head of the personnel department, screens the list of nominees along with the names suggested by participants (the title used for protégés) to make the initial matches and to build a pool of available mentors for later additions to the professional staff.

Using Nomination by Protégés. In the GAO (R. Glazer, interview by author, 1989), the mentoring program is administered by a panel that asks the candidates (protégés) to nominate three people whom they would like to consider as their senior adviser (mentor). When one of the three is matched with a candidate, the other two may be asked to be members of the mentor pool and be considered by other candidates. In this way the pool of potential mentors is expanded as the number of active relationships grows.

Making It Workable and Rewarding for Mentors

Select the Title for the Role of Mentor. Your choice will be based on how you structure the mentor role and on the organization's culture: in turn, the term you use will influence how the role is carried out. For example, *exemplar* suggests that the mentor may be expected only to model behaviors for the protégé. The term *coach* implies that the mentor will be involved in specific skills-training activities. Some organizations are comfortable with the term *mentor*, while others think it is too trendy for their own programs. The term must be one that most people in the organization can be comfortable with, particularly the mentors themselves.

Describe the Responsibilities. Make the description factual and realistic. It is tempting to make the mentoring role sound glamorous, which can raise some unrealistic expectations about the benefits. Include in this description the number of protégés the mentor is expected to work with at any one time. As noted in Chapter Seven, I recommend one mentor to one protégé unless the mentor is extraordinarily skilled and has a lot of surplus time. Specify the type and frequency of reporting that will be required, if any. Include an estimate of the time the mentor may be expected to spend in developmental activities with the protégé.

Advertise. Develop promotional pieces suitable to the communication vehicles available to you to publicize the existence, features, and benefits of your mentoring program. Soliciting volunteers necessitates spreading the word as widely as possible. Consider word of mouth, daily bulletins, periodic newsletters, union newspapers, management reports, training catalogs, and desk-drop leaflets. Publish the endorsement of the program by high-level administrators or managers.

Make It Easy to Respond. Prepare a simple form for volunteers or nominators to use. The amount and type of information you require will vary depending on the structure of your program and the size of your organization. You want enough information to make it relatively easy to match the mentor's experience and capabilities with the protégé's developmental needs. Ask for at the least this much information:

- Name
- Current location
- Education
- Experience
- Why interested in the mentor role
- Type of mentoring relationship wanted
- Amount of time available for mentoring activities
- Any constraints on location or timing

Screen Candidates for Readiness. Amend the hallmarks of master mentors at the beginning of this chapter and use it as an initial screening checklist to assess the readiness of the volunteers and nominees for the mentor pool.

Make the Match with the Protégé. A review of the preliminary development plans of the protégés will reveal the precise experience and skills sought in the mentors. Mentor candidates who have passed the initial screening can be contacted for additional information—skills, experience, abilities, and availability—that is relevant to the needs of a specific person who is seeking a mentor.

Making It Work

Orient Mentors to the Role. A group orientation session may be most efficient when the program is first established. Later it may be practical to have the coordinator brief the new mentors individually. A sample outline for a mentor orientation session is included in Chapter Eleven.

Make It Matter to the Mentors. The rewards you offer will have a major impact on the mentors' motivation. Some of the ways you can build rewards into your program were described in Chapter Five. The surest way to cause the mentor to take the role seriously is to tie the mentor's performance to the regular appraisal process. This performance objective can then be negotiated with the mentor's boss and tracked for progress and feedback. The protégé can be a valuable source of feedback on the quality and timeliness of the mentor's performance. Financial rewards may be in the form of bonuses, stock options, or paid time off. Nonfinancial, yet visible and powerful, rewards include trips, featured recognition in publications, certificates, attendance at special educational programs, and tickets for entertainment events. Do not underestimate the power of a gold star!

Maintain Records on the Mentor Pool. If your organization has established a personnel database, use it to keep track of volunteers or nominees. This database can be used later to track the relationship after matches have been made.

Checklist

The potential for your program to succeed can be increased by careful recruitment and selection of mentors. Use Exhibit 3 to jot down specific actions you can take to ensure a good structure. Be realistic and specific in the actions you plan to take.

**Exhibit 3. Checklist for Structuring the Mentor Role
and Creating the Mentor Pool.**

Action to Take

1. What term will we use for the
   mentor role?

2. How will we recruit mentors?

3. What are the basic characteristics
   we want mentors to have?

4. How will we reward mentors?

5. How will we use promotional
   material to attract mentors?

6. How can we make it easy for
   people to volunteer or respond
   to the nomination process?

7. What process will we use to
   screen the mentor candidates'
   skills:
   —general?
   —relationship specific?

8. What systems do we have or need
   to record and maintain the
   mentor pool?

9. What will we include in the
   description of the mentor's role?

10. How can we ensure that mentors
    share credit with protégés?

11. How can we ensure that mentors
    let protégés take the risks
    necessary for learning?

12. How will we orient mentors to
    the role?

13. _____

14. _____

9

Selecting Protégés and Diagnosing Their Development Needs

One of the most frequently cited and important benefits of facilitating mentoring is the increased likelihood of success for the protégé. Achievement is one of the key motivators. When you can ensure success through the guidance of a mentor, the enthusiasm and motivation of the protégé are sustained. In addition, because protégés have fewer failure exercises than people who are not protégés, the organization's cost for grooming talented people to take on different or increased responsibility is reduced. This chapter will help you identify the protégé group, screen and select the protégés, and diagnose and make plans to meet their specific needs.

Identifying Protégé Candidates

Chapter Seven discussed the use of succession-planning techniques to identify major protégé target groups. For example, an organization in which many executives will retire in the near future might target second-line managers who have the potential to move up. If necessitated by the organization's affirmative-action goals, this target group might be further narrowed to women and minorities in lower level positions.

After determining the target group, the task is to identify

118

individuals who will do well in a facilitated mentoring program. The most popular strategies used to locate the candidates are self-nomination, boss nomination, and sponsor nomination.

Self-Nomination. Perhaps the easiest way to identify protégés is to issue a call for self-nominations. Those who nominate themselves are likely to be motivated and capable of self-directed growth.

When using this strategy, it is important to communicate clearly the criteria for participation, responsibilities, and expected outcomes of the program. For example, the TRAC program (see Chapter Six) clearly states in its application form that to volunteer one must, among other things, be a TRAC member in good standing, abide by the Statement of Mentee Responsibilities, and not take any financial reimbursement for participation in the program.

Failure to make criteria and conditions clear is likely to create a horrendous work load for the program coordinator. For example, Trinity College (see Chapter Six) found that excluding any student who planned to study abroad in her junior year reduced the number of applicants by 50 percent. This new criterion made administration of the program easier than it had been because it ensured that the mentoring relationship would not be interrupted by students' travel, and it reduced the number of applications that had to be processed and the number of relationships that had to be monitored.

Stating protégé criteria serves another important purpose. It can save you the task of telling those self-nominated candidates who are not ready that they are not viable candidates for the program. Explicitly stating all criteria for the program before announcing that people may volunteer often prevents having unqualified people apply.

Boss Nomination. The second strategy for identifying protégés also requires that objectives and criteria for participation be clearly and widely publicized. With the strategy of boss nomination, managers and supervisors are invited to nominate candidates to participate in the program. The succession-

planning group could also issue a request that people be identified who have the potential for promotion in specific areas. The
request may be made openly through memos, management
bulletins, newsletters. If the program is not open to everyone,
direction for nomination of protégés may come from operating
officers to managers at the next tier in closed meetings, confidential memoranda, or personal conversations.

Keep in mind that bosses often have blind spots as to the
potential of their subordinates. If you have any concern that
some managers or supervisors may be less than enthusiastic
about nominating their own people, the program coordinator
can make direct contacts with bosses to encourage the development of their people.

Sponsor Nomination. The third strategy, sponsor nomination, avoids the blind spots or biases of bosses. It allows any
astute observer to nominate a candidate. Input can come from
leaders in every function of the organization. However, if you are
looking for a particular set of protégé experiences, skills, and
interests, the coordinator might best go only to managers or
administrators of the most relevant function. For example, if the
succession-planning group has forecast significant opportunity
for growth in new markets, additional sales managers will be
needed. In this case, perhaps only the current marketing or sales
managers will be asked to nominate high-potential people in
their divisions.

Whichever strategy you choose, criteria for participating
in the program must be made available to every possible source
of protégé candidates. Exhibit 4 is a sample call for participants
using all three strategies.

Selection Processes

Once a group of potential protégés is identified, a process
of selection and matching takes place. In today's equal-
opportunity environment, training and development programs
are supposedly open to all. But strategies for protégé selection

Exhibit 4. Sample Call for Protégé Candidates.

Facilitated Mentoring Program

Candidates are invited to participate in a program to develop specific skills and experiences in a targeted, facilitated interaction with a mentor. Nominations can be made by the following people:

- Anyone who wishes to participate may nominate him/herself.
- Bosses may nominate their subordinates who have the potential to grow and develop additional skills.
- Candidates may be nominated by any manager or supervisor who has had experience with assessment of the potential of the candidate.

---

can be biased. Problems cited in the selection process (Myers and Humphreys, 1985) include preselection, use of an old-boy network, nepotism, and outright discrimination. For example, when mentors are able to nominate protégés, they may secretly select a person and then manipulate the matching process to ensure that they get their choice. Or alert protégés may observe the power structure and choose mentors who can provide them with the best entry into an old-boy network.

In a free-enterprise economy, ownership carries the right to allocate all resources, including development programs. The owners of firms often give favorable treatment to family members and friends. Nepotism has long been an accepted way of building businesses and ensuring continuity of leadership. Many entrepreneurs involve family members in their businesses to get them off the ground. Such favorable treatment becomes troublesome when it is practiced by managers who are not owners. Sometimes executives trade favors with executives in other areas. The vice-president of finance asks the vice-president of marketing to give a relative a summer job. Or the comptroller asks the chief of personnel to make an internship available for a subordinate of the comptroller.

Discrimination in selection of people for special development programs has hurt women and minorities especially. There are still few women and minorities in high-level, powerful positions. Overtly unfair practices in selection of protégés will

result in discrimination suits. The subtle unfairnesses are difficult to control, yet they can be minimized with a carefully
crafted selection process.

How you establish the policy and procedures for selection
and matching of protégés to mentors can feed or thwart such
undesirable practices. A good example of fair practice can be
found at General Electric's Power Generation Division, where
mentoring is a vital part of the training for new field engineers
(O'Reilly, 1989). Each trainee (their term for the protégé) is
assigned two mentors. The second one is there to help orient the
new engineer if, for whatever reason, the first relationship does
not work. Such fail-safe mechanisms can ensure that a protégé
receives fair treatment during the developmental process.

I discuss next a few criteria for protégés that you might
consider when designing your selection process. All of them will
help maximize the positive experience of the protégés.

The primary criterion for selection is that the protégé be
motivated to develop different or greater competencies. No
matter how formally or informally the relationship is structured,
if the protégé is not motivated, nothing will be gained. Facilitated programs work because protégés actively pursue new
learning.

The characteristics and responsibilities of participants at
Rooney, Ida, Nolt and Ahern are described in Exhibit 5.

Other criteria for protégé selection include the ability to
perform in more than one functional area and the assessed
potential to perform at least two levels above the present position in the organization. Similar criteria must be established for
your program based on its goals and the target population.

➤   *Look for the curious individual who is demanding more training*
     and new assignments.

Motivated individuals are also likely to take personal
responsibility for their own growth and development. Mentoring removes the responsibility for skill development from the
organization and puts it squarely on the shoulders of the individual, where it belongs. There must therefore be a great com-

Exhibit 5. Sample of Announced Characteristics of Protégés.

---

*Characteristics and Responsibilities of Participants in the
Rooney, Ida, Nolt and Ahern Mentoring Program*

It is expected that participants in the mentoring program will have
these characteristics:

- Goal oriented
- Willingness to assume responsibility for one's own growth and
  development
- Actively seeks challenging assignment and greater responsibility
- Receptive to feedback and coaching

Responsibilities will include:

- Identifying developmental needs and setting development goals
- Formulating an action plan for accomplishing goals
- Maintenance of individual development plan documentation
- Regular contact with the coordinator on the progress of the
  relationship

Source: Rooney, Ida, Nolt and Ahern, 1989. Used with permission.

mitment on the part of the protégé to assume responsibility for
his or her own development. "That concept of individual responsibility for career development is an integral part of the
training philosophy at Glendale Federal Savings and Loan"
(Hogan, 1984). The strategy of self-nomination will most likely
yield the most protégé candidates who are willing to take responsibility for their own development. When the selection is
initially made by sponsors, you cannot make this assumption.

➡️   *Look for a person who initiates a career-development plan and
frequently participates in outside workshops and seminars.*

Making Plans to Meet Developmental Needs

Diagnosing Needs. Development activities are best targeted to specific, diagnosed needs. Ways to diagnose developmental needs range from using formal, external diagnostic
centers to relying on the protégé's own gut feeling of what she or
he wants. The General Accounting Office (GAO) has used an

assessment center where protégé candidates take part in simulated business activities, in-basket exercises, employee discussion scenarios, and problem-solving cases. The candidates get feedback on their progress and an assessment of their specific developmental needs.

However, when gathering data for this section of the book and in our discussions with people in a wide variety of organizations, we found few who use assessment centers, either internal or external. The popularity of formal assessment centers appears to be waning, while use of assessment instruments is growing. This increase may be due to the growing body of research that validates these tools. The instruments also tend to be far less costly and less cumbersome to administer than participation in an assessment center.

A survey of assessment instruments was published by *Training Magazine* (Zemke, 1982). The categories ranged from assessing managerial/leadership style to aptitude assessment. Exhibitors at every professional conference display a wide variety of resources for assessing skills, communication styles, behaviors, personality types, and learning styles. Every day our mail contains brochures about new instruments and assessment tools. You will certainly have no difficulty finding a wide selection of these instruments. The difficulty will be in narrowing your choices to those that fit your needs and are practical to use in your environment.

Here is a brief description of a few of the assessment instruments that could be used to diagnose developmental needs of protégés in a mentoring program. This list is far from complete and is not meant as an endorsement of these above other similar instruments. The resource section of this book contains complete information on the publishers of each of these instruments.

The Personal Profile System©, marketed by Carlson Learning Company, is a work-behavior assessment profile that can assist the participant in identifying similarities and differences in mentor and protégé work-behavior patterns. It displays the primary tendencies of Dominance, Steadiness, Influencing of Others, and Compliance (to their standards) of the respondent. In addition to the primary tendencies, behaviors are described more precisely for the respondent in graphs illustrating three of the fifteen Classical Profile Patterns.

Another self-rating process, this one with ten "personal-growth" skills areas, is Managing Personal Growth© (Blessing/White). The indicators assessed with this tool are: knowing what you want from life; having a realistic sense of personal strengths and weaknesses; making decisions and setting priorities with good judgment; initiating action; generating new ideas and alternative solutions; anticipating and seizing opportunities; planning; getting support from others; learning; and being optimistic, decisive, flexible, purposeful, motivated, enthusiastic, assertive, confident.

ACUMEN: Insight for Managers (human synergistics®) is a software adaptation of the Life Styles Inventory designed and normed for managers. According to the descriptive literature this instrument "develops managers' abilities to understand and communicate with a variety of individuals."

SKILLSCOPE© (Center for Creative Leadership) assesses managers' strengths and developmental needs. Ninety-eight skills are assessed in major classes such as information exchange, interpersonal relationships, influence (both taking and accepting), decision making, and use of self. The instrument must be completed by the respondent and five to eight of the respondent's coworkers.

The Personal Skills Map© (Nelson and Low, Life Skills Center) is a self-marking, self-scoring instrument that measures eleven career and life-effectiveness skills on fourteen scales: Self-Esteem, Assertion, Interpersonal Comfort, Empathy, Drive Strength, Decision Making, Time Management, Sales Orientation, Commitment Ethic, Stress Management, and Physical Wellness. The respondent's personal communication style is assessed on scales of Interpersonal Assertion, Interpersonal Aggression, and Interpersonal Deference. The degree of satisfaction with current skill levels is assessed on the scale of Personal-Change Orientation. This instrument is particularly useful for establishing a baseline of these career effectiveness skills prior to beginning the development program. At an appropriate interval following practice of the skills it can be taken again to measure and evaluate the degree of change.

➤   *Look for tools and processes that fit the need, are valid, reliable, and easy to use by coordinators, mentors, and protégés.*

Preparing an Individual Development Plan. It will take more than a word of encouragement to make the protégé responsible for his or her own development. Protégés must have a development plan based on diagnosed needs and supported by adequate resources.

Before any developmental plan can be completed, however, the amount of time the protégé can dedicate to mentoring activities as opposed to "the real job" must be determined. Mentoring activities may be totally on company time, the protégé's own time, or a combination of the two. In practice, the time spent in developmental activities is most often in addition to the regular job for both mentor and protégé.

Once the desired skills and experiences are known and how the time will be handled has been agreed on, the development plan can be drafted. The development plan can be as simple as a few lines on a card that serve as the basis for discussion between the mentor and protégé. It can also be a multipage form that records planned activities for several months or years. Ideally the development plan will use the same format as that used for performance planning, objective setting, and action planning. The documented details will include projected outcomes, time lines, resources required, and progress checkpoints. The key is to make it work for the protégé, rather than consuming a lot of effort to maintain the document.

Exhibit 6 is a sample of guidelines for the protégé to use in preparing an initial development plan. Exhibit 7 is a sample form for planning and tracking developmental activities. After the initial drafting by the protégé, the document can be refined by all interested parties. In the Executive Candidate Development Program (General Accounting Office), the candidate designs an eighteen-month development plan, which is reviewed

Exhibit 6. Sample Development Plan Guidelines.

Each goal will be recorded on a separate Development Plan sheet. Your goals may be professional, educational, and personal. Some examples include marketing results, advancement, staff recruitment, chargeable hours, and development of special skills. The Development Plan is to be completed by the participant. Spaces are provided for:

Name:	(yours)
Date:	Date by which you expect to have accomplished the goal.
Development Goal:	In this space write the goal you wish to achieve. Make the statement in terms of the outcome, or end result, rather than the process you will use to get there.
Action Steps:	List detailed, sequential steps for how to achieve this goal.
Target Dates:	For each action step, enter a target date for completion of the step. Pencil these dates in your daily planner to help keep on schedule.
Resources Required:	You may need assistance from other than your mentor. List people, places, funds, and any other items you anticipate needing to accomplish each action.
Status/Progress Comments:	Use this column to prepare for discussion with your mentor and for reinforcing yourself for completing scheduled action steps. Enter comments about the status of each action, progress made since the last review, etc.
	When appropriate, note concerns that you wish to discuss with your mentor. Enter date of discussion.
	Add Action Steps and additional target dates when appropriate.

---

by the boss, the mentor, and the Resources Board (see Chapter Six).

Should the natural boss be included in the approval of the development plan? It depends on the organization. In some cases, the natural boss's responsibility is for job and task functions only and does not include career-development planning. A good example can be found in a typical accounting firm, where staff is assigned to a manager for a two- to six-month audit

Exhibit 7. Sample Development Plan Form.

Name: _____

Date: _____

Development Goal:

Action Steps	Target Dates	Resources Required	Status/Progress Comments

To whom will I communicate accomplishment of this goal?_____

project. The manager will probably have little interest in the long-term career development of young accountants or auditors on the team. The focus is on getting the audit completed. Long-term developmental planning is often the responsibility of a partner or of the personnel administrator. In such a case, the manager would be involved in the development plans of team members only if some of the activities were to be carried out during the time of the audit.

In contrast, most industry assignments at the management level run from two to five years. In these environments the natural boss is usually aware of the importance of including development plans with other planned objectives. The long duration of the boss/subordinate relationship in these organizations makes it easy to look for opportunities and projects that will result in the protégé learning new skills.

➤   *Find or design a simple development plan form that provides a record of skills and experiences to be gained, types of learning activities to be pursued, and an approximate time frame for completing the planned activities.*

Checklist

That gives you some of the how-tos of identifying and selecting protégés, diagnosing developmental needs, and devising development plans. You can prepare for these processes by answering the questions on the checklist in Exhibit 8.

Exhibit 8. Checklist for Identifying and Selecting Protégés and Making Plans to Meet Their Developmental Needs.

	Action to Take
1. What term will we use for the role of protégé?	
2. How will candidates for protégé be nominated?	

**Exhibit 8. Checklist for Identifying and Selecting Protégés
and Making Plans to Meet Their Developmental Needs, Cont'd.**

---

3. What criteria will we use to select
   individuals into the mentoring
   program?

4. What will be the balance of time
   commitments to the protégé's
   core job and to development
   activities?

5. What steps will we take to
   encourage protégés to take
   responsibility for their own
   growth and development?

6. What processes or tools will be
   used to diagnose the
   developmental needs of the
   protégé?

7. What format should the
   development plan have?

8. Who should have a part in
   reviewing the development plan?

9. What can protégés expect,
   realistically, about promotion?

10. What agreements about the use
    of the mentor's and protégé's
    time will we recommend?

11. How will we orient the protégés
    to their role?

12. _____

13. _____

14. _____

10

Involving the Boss
Who Is Not the Mentor

How will the natural boss of the protégé react to having a subordinate involved in a mentoring relationship? This concern is frequently raised when someone other than the protégé's direct-line supervisor functions as a mentor. Indeed, this triangle can present a number of problems, which I discuss in this chapter along with possible solutions.

Objections Raised by Natural Bosses

The boss who is not good at developing subordinates may not understand the nature of the protégé's development activities. For example, the boss may be suspicious and resentful of the subordinate taking the time to go to a meeting that is seemingly unrelated to the protégé's current assignment, not understanding that the purpose of attending is to observe and learn good techniques for leading meetings. A boss with this perception of mentoring activities is also overlooking the fact that the skill building that is taking place may benefit the protégé's regular job performance as well.

Jealousy and insecurity are other potential problems. Quite often, the protégé's mentor is at a higher level in the organization than the boss. Suddenly, the subordinate has access to information and networks that the boss doesn't have. The boss begins to feel inadequate or left out.

131

Other bosses lack a belief in development programs of any sort. Most managers and administrators still feel that getting the immediate job done right is the only priority. This belief is evidenced by the inevitable cancellation of a planned training course when there is any risk of failing to meet production schedules. Bosses who believe that they are letting protégés off for "extra" development assignments will view time away from the job as a cost rather than an investment.

Some bosses who are not committed to development programs think that people should have all the required skills and abilities when they take a job. In reality, even in the best of labor situations it is unusual to find the mix of skills necessary to match perfectly the requirements of an open position. And, in employment boom times, when only 2 to 5 percent of the work force is considered unemployed, it is rare to find those with the skills needed for many jobs.

In addition, some bosses lack a commitment specifically to the mentoring program: "I got here through my own hard work and initiative. Why should we give special attention to young employees?"

Overcoming Objections and Gaining Commitment

It is necessary to build into your design some mechanisms that will prevent the insecure boss from undermining the program. How do you get agreement and support from the boss? Here are some suggestions.

Plan for Shared Responsibility Between the Mentor and the Boss. The current boss knows how the protégé is performing on the job and can make valuable suggestions for the protégé's development plan, which should include activities for strengthening skills required to perform effectively in the current job as well as for acquiring skills needed for the future. When the agreement is negotiated between the mentor and protégé, the boss can provide suggestions and information ahead of time or be an active participant in the discussion. In the Executive Candidate Development Program (General Accounting Office), the supervisor has input at several steps in the process. Input is given at the initial nomination, at the point of planning development activities, and prior to the final progress-review meeting. In addition, as the boss will have much more opportunity to observe the protégé's day-to-day performance than will the mentor, it follows that the boss will have more opportunities to provide feedback and coaching. By being a part of the process in these ways, the boss will have a stake in the protégé's success and will become an interested, committed party to the process.

If the boss is in the best position to know and observe the protégé, why shouldn't the boss be the formal mentor? In a sense, all bosses should be doing informal mentoring of their subordinates for the skills required for the particular job. However, the goal of most mentoring programs is to broaden the skills of the protégé. I have discussed previously that an advantage of having a mentor from another function is that it provides the protégé with a new perspective. Some evidence also indicates that bosses who act as mentors for their subordinates have a hard time letting go of the relationship. In one health care environment (Darling, 1985), sour endings to the mentoring relationship were found to be more likely with bosses who had a position of authority over their protégés than with those who were not direct bosses. Finally, not all bosses have the skills that good mentors need.

➤ *Structure the development plan to allow for both boss and mentor input.*

Plan for Interaction Between the Boss and the Mentor. This planned interaction can diffuse the concern of the boss about the protégé's being involved in a special relationship with another, perhaps higher-level, manager. At Merrill Lynch (Farren, Gray, and Kaye, 1984) the mentor is encouraged to call each protégé's manager and become acquainted. The mentor works with four protégés during a six-month period, and both the mentor and the protégés keep the managers apprised of what they're doing.

The coordinator may also convene periodic meetings of

the boss, mentor, and protégé to discuss the progress of the development plan. If periodic meetings are typically scheduled with mentors only, the bosses can be included occasionally. It would be relatively easy to design some exercises for those meetings to guide the boss and mentor in a discussion of the protégé's progress and further developmental needs.

One word of caution. When the mentor and boss are interacting regularly, the protégé may be uncomfortable discussing confidential issues with the mentor, particularly if they concern issues or problems that involve the boss. The mentor must be prepared to keep the protégé's trust and deal with such private information in a diplomatic, sensitive way.

➤　　*Look for ways to bring the boss, mentor, and protégé together on a regular basis.*

Communicate to the Boss That Performance Planning and Feedback Are Easier When a Subordinate Is a Protégé. Initial anxiety and fears of losing control may obscure an important benefit for the boss. The boss's job can be made easier when the protégé is taking full responsibility for the tasks of preparing and executing a development plan. Further, as the protégé is praised for carrying out these tasks, they will transfer to the day-to-day job. An alert boss can reinforce that behavior by commending the employee for taking the initiative in performance planning and tracking of progress.

Let the boss know about such benefits in the material you use to promote the program. Stress the fact that the protégé's development plan can be tied to regular performance plans. The coordinator can also tell bosses of such benefits during the protégé nomination and selection process.

➤　　*Communicate to the boss the benefits of having a subordinate who is in a mentoring relationship.*

Alert the Boss to Opportunities to Learn About People Development. The boss who is not a world-class supervisor has an opportunity to learn valuable skills for managing people by observing how a competent mentor interacts with a protégé. While never having to admit the lack of those particular skills, the boss can watch them modeled by the mentor, then imitate them in performance planning and feedback discussions with the protégé and other subordinates.

➤ *Alert the boss to opportunities to watch the mentor work with people.*

Use the Program to Make the Boss Aware of the Benefits of Human Resource Development. Line managers are often skeptical of the value of development activities. They see human resources as a costly staff function that has questionable results. With facilitated mentoring, the program coordinator has an opportunity to consult with the boss and get support for all development programs. The mentoring program should be presented as one component of the total program rather than as a separate function. Ideally, as a result, the boss will become a stakeholder in all development functions. Instead of being an adversary, the boss will see the whole program as a potential resource for development of all subordinates.

➤ *Look for a way to build a bridge between the boss and the human-resource staff.*

Checklist

What other ideas do you have for strategies for involving the boss of a protégé? Use the checklist in Exhibit 9 to come up with your own action items.

Exhibit 9. Checklist for Involving the Natural Boss.

	Action to Take
1. How will the natural boss provide input to the protégé's development plan?	_____ _____ _____

Exhibit 9. Checklist for Involving the Natural Boss, Cont'd.

2. How will the natural boss be involved with the mentor?　　_____

3. What will we do to gain commitment from the natural boss?　　_____

4. How will the protégé build development activities into the regular job?　　_____

5. How can we encourage the natural boss to learn from the mentor?　　_____

6. How can the coordinator build the boss's confidence in human-resource programs and the mentoring process?　　_____

7. _____

8. _____

9. _____

11

The Coordinator: Selection, Training, and Responsibilities

Coordination is central to the success of facilitated mentoring. The coordinator orchestrates all the elements of the program. In most instances, the coordinator is a permanent employee, usually someone with other duties in human resources or personnel. Small organizations, or those with small pilot programs, might consider contracting this function out.

In general, the coordinator assists in the selection, assessment, matching, and orientation of mentors and protégés. Additional responsibilities can be assigned to the coordinator depending on the nature and structure of the program. Essentially, the coordinator is a relationship manager who sees that the needs of the mentor, protégé, and organization are met. This chapter includes specific guidelines for structuring the coordinator role.

Selection

Before you begin to think about the mechanics of coordination, it is useful to review the reasons why you want a facilitated mentoring program in the first place. If you are in a corporate setting, your organization more than likely has a specific succession-planning goal. You want to have sufficient people ready now to fill all projected staffing requirements. You are looking for more than just warm bodies. You want people with relevant skills for each of the projected positions. It is unlikely you will be able to locate and hire people who already have those skills, so you must facilitate the growth and development of the organization's people. Your decision may be to structure a mentoring program to meet that goal.

If your organization has placed a high priority on the mentoring program, the next major decision is whom you will select as coordinator. The multifaceted job of the coordinator is a most critical one for a facilitated mentoring program. Don't put a junior person with minimal skills in the coordinator role.

In a corporate environment the coordinator must have up-to-date knowledge of the business plan and all supporting strategic plans. In a government agency the coordinator needs to know, at the least, the projections for staff and the anticipated budget for training and development. In a nonprofit group the coordinator might need to know the numbers and ratios of paid professionals and volunteers on the staff. Even more importantly, the coordinator in any organization must have the respect and cooperation of the top people. Without this respect and considerable skills, it will be impossible for the coordinator to mediate sensitive discussions and resolve them effectively.

You must also look at how many coordinators your program needs. To some extent this number may be determined by the total number of people in the organization. More precisely, it will be influenced by the number of people who will be involved in mentor/protégé relationships at any given time. If a program is small, this function can be handled in addition to other human-resource responsibilities, such as recruitment, placement, training, and development. It is dangerous to overload a coordinator, however. The coordinator must be able to give high priority to preventing potential problems and resolving those problems that do come up. Exhibit 10 describes the role of the coordinator in a small organization. Use the description to gauge the number of coordinators your program will need.

Exhibit 10. Sample Coordinator Responsibilities.

The basic responsibility of the program coordinator is to facilitate the successful growth of people in the organization. The coordinator is a primary resource to protégés and mentors and may be contacted with any questions about the mentoring program. Specific functions of the coordinator are described briefly in the following section.

Maintaining Mentor Pool	The goal is to have an adequate pool of mentors to make appropriate matches with protégés on a timely basis. The coordinator periodically requests volunteers, invites protégés to nominate their preferences of mentors, ar ' receives recommendations from department managers and other firm leaders.

1. Recruiting
   a. A call for nominations will be extended two times each year. Protégés will nominate five candidates each as potential mentors.
   b. As needed, the coordinator will request volunteers and ask for recommendations from department managers and other firm leaders.
   c. Volunteers may advise coordinator of interest and availability at any time. For example, a new hire with a particular expertise.
2. Screen and Match
   a. A matrix of mentor/protégé relationships is maintained.
   b. The coordinator interacts with department heads and firm leaders to determine the most appropriate match of mentors and protégés.
   c. The coordinator may be contacted by either mentor or protégé to develop a new match. For example, the protégé attains all goals set with the current mentor and wishes to develop in another area.

Assisting with Development Goals	Regularly assess areas for growth and development of potential protégés.

1. Review personnel files for indicators of particular strengths and needs.
2. Review recent self-evaluations.
3. Analyze recent assessments of skills, behaviors, and styles.

Exhibit 10. Sample Coordinator Responsibilities, Cont'd.

Negotiating the Agreement	Typically the mentor and protégé will negotiate the specifics of their agreement. The coordinator is available to participate in the discussion when appropriate. The coordinator will provide possible agreement and development-plan formats.
Conducting Meetings	The coordinator conducts group meetings of mentors and protégés when appropriate.
Conducting Mentor Orientation	The coordinator conducts mentor orientations according to guidelines provided.
Conducting Protégé Orientation	The coordinator conducts protégé orientations according to guidelines provided.
Maintaining Records	Involvement in the program is noted in mentor and protégé personnel files.

Responsibilities

The following point-by-point discussion of coordinator responsibilities will help those of you who are selecting coordinators and those coordinators who want to get a good grasp of their responsibilities.

Facilitating Growth of Protégés. As with mentors, a primary consideration is to find coordinators who care about the growth and development of others because most of their time will be spent looking out for someone else's needs. They must be good listeners who can judge a person's motivation level and personal needs. They must also be quick to sense problems that surface during the mentoring relationship. Often such problems are unspoken—they are manifested in a protégé's body language or in unreturned phone calls to the mentor. Coordinators must be able to pick up such cues, analyze them, and act quickly. To do so, they must be skilled in:

- Coaching
- Counseling
- Communicating with appropriate assertiveness

- Negotiating
- Giving feedback

The coordinator acts as a coach to all parties in the mentoring process from the initial screening of mentors to the dissolution of the relationship. Many situations call for coaching. For example, the coordinator may coach both the mentor and protégé in preparing to negotiate their agreement.

In addition, finely honed counseling skills are necessary in routine and unusual circumstances. The coordinator must be equally prepared to counsel the protégé who is frustrated with a career and the one who confesses a sexual attraction to the mentor.

Appropriately assertive communication skills are useful to the coordinator in such situations—and critical when an issue in the relationship has escalated to the point where the coordinator is sought out to resolve it. Similarly, negotiation skills are called for in every activity from the building of the initial, hopeful agreement to the termination of the disappointing one.

Good feedback skills are musts for coordinators. The ability to recognize what type of feedback is relevant to each person and in each situation, and to give feedback that reinforces desired behavior, is one of the most valuable skills for keeping mentoring relationships on the positive side.

→   *Look for a diplomat to fill the coordinator role.*

Analyzing Jobs, Tasks, Needs. Coordinators must also have good, practical analysis skills. For starters, they must be able to analyze jobs and tasks and determine what kind of abilities and experience a position requires. Assessment of the protégé's developmental needs is another key skill for coordinators. If you plan to use any developmental diagnostic instruments, such as those for assessing skills, patterns of work behaviors, or personality, the coordinators must have extensive background in the theoretical research on and application of such instruments. Training and practice in the administration and interpretation of the selected tools is an essential part of the preparation of the coordinators for their role.

➡️   *Look for a coordinator with a background in research and performance technology.*

Promoting the Program. The coordinator must be able to design and develop exciting promotional materials to attract participants. At the same time, these materials must present the program specifics accurately so that only qualified participants apply. This is the challenge for a good public-relations writer.

➡️   *Look for a person skillful at writing and marketing.*

Coordinating Multiple Activities. The coordinator or coordination staff administers all elements of the mentoring program. Some nitty-gritty record keeping is involved, as well as the fascinating aspects of being in on advance planning for the organization. The models in Chapter Six illustrate the many components of various types of programs. At a minimum, the coordinator is in charge of:

- Protégé identification
- Mentor-candidate screening
- Matching mentor with protégé
- Conducting orientation programs
- Negotiating agreements
- Tracking the health of the relationships
- Evaluating the effectiveness of the program

➡️   *Look for people with strong administrative skills.*

Gaining and Maintaining the Commitment of Top Management. Occasionally, the program may come under scrutiny or may suffer when top management forgets to make it a priority. When emotions run high, the coordinator must have sufficient clout to work problems out with top managers. And the coordinator must be able to keep the program visible.

➡️ *Give the coordinator authority and status.*

Working with an Advisory Board. It may be advantageous to select an advisory board made up of representatives from every function in the organization to create policy and to provide guidance to the program coordinator. When the leaders of all functions are held responsible for the program, support is built in from the beginning. A panel or group of advisers brings a broad range of knowledge about the future direction of the organization and is an excellent source of information about future job opportunities.

Such a board exists in the Executive Candidate Development Program (ECDP), U.S. General Accounting Office (GAO), as illustrated in Chapter Six. "The Executive Resources Board (ERB) is responsible for the structure, content, and operation [of the program], inclusive of assessing needs for executives, initiating new ECDP classes and making recommendations concerning which senior level managers should be selected into the program" (Glazer and Murray, 1990). The ERB is directly involved in all aspects of the program, with the following tasks and responsibilities:

- Approves mentors for each of the candidates (protégés)
- Reviews and approves each candidate's proposed development plan
- Monitors and assesses each candidate's progress and performance throughout the length of the program
- Advises candidates on suggested changes to the development plan
- Makes judgments on program certification
- Makes placement decisions at the conclusion of the program
- Makes decisions about program structure and content

Coordinators must be able to use advisory boards for support and useful advice. They must be willing to share the responsibility and to make visible use of the evaluations and recommendations that the board makes.

➤   *Select a coordinator who accepts and uses feedback.*

Matching Mentor and Protégé. Previous chapters described the need to carefully match protégés and mentors using objective criteria based on the protégés' developmental needs and the ability of the mentors to act as resources for fulfilling those needs. At every step of the way, the coordinator must be sure that roles are clear and that the match is appropriate. For an open program in a fairly large organization, the tasks of the coordinator in matching and preparing the mentor and protégé for their mentoring relationship are described in this way (adapted from Murray-Hicks, 1972):

1.   The lead coordinator for a mentor/protégé pair will be one with an established relationship with the mentor. Another coordinator will be an alternate contact.
2.   The coordinator contacts the mentor to advise of potential selection.
3.   Coordinator and mentor candidate meet to:
     a.   Describe the Facilitated Mentoring Program
     b.   Assess commitment of mentor candidate
     c.   Gain indication of match to protégé
4.   Notify matched mentor and other potential mentors of the status of their selection.
5.   Meet with selected mentor individually to:
     a.   Brief on protégé biography
     b.   Assign orientation pre-work if appropriate: Personal Skills Map©, Personal Profile System©
     c.   Schedule orientation for mentor

6. Meet with protégé individually to:
   a. Brief on mentor biography
   b. Assign orientation pre-work if appropriate: Personal Skills Map©, Personal Profile System©
   c. Schedule orientation for protégé

➤ *Look for a coordinator who pays attention to detail.*

Designing Orientations. How the mentors and protégés are oriented to their roles and responsibilities will directly influence how they relate to each other and how they carry out the development activities. The coordinator usually has the responsibility of designing the orientation to fit the policies and structure of the specific program. The coordinator has to be astute at assessing the best way to meet the needs of mentors and protégés. For example, when you start your program it may be most effective to conduct a group orientation for all mentors. As the program continues and additional people assume the mentor role, it may be convenient for the coordinator to do individual orientations. Another option is to have a top-notch mentor orient the new one, a sort-of peer mentoring.

Similarly, the orientation for protégés who are already employed but new to a mentoring relationship will differ from that for those new employees who will go directly into a mentoring relationship. When you have an established mentoring program that is available to everyone, the regular orientation to the organization and the job can include the features and responsibilities of the mentoring relationships.

At the least, the coordinator needs to structure orientations and find the appropriate people to run them. In most cases, the coordinator conducts the orientations. Exhibits 11 and 12 illustrate the types of activities that might take place in mentor and protégé group orientations. Exhibit 13 is the outline for an individual orientation of protégés in an open-to-all mentoring program at a small firm.

➤ *Look for a coordinator who has experience in structuring and facilitating group activities.*

Exhibit 11. Sample Outline for Group Orientation of Mentors.

Activity	Process/Resources
Self-assessment of generic career and life skills	Personal Skills Map© (PSM)
Recognizing human motivation needs	Presentation
Researching mission, values, and culture of organization	Group process
Mentoring process as component of human-resource development, staffing requirements, and succession plans	Presentation
Roles of the four parties in the Facilitated Mentoring Program	Presentation/ discussion
Identifying individual work behavior patterns (if not done as pre-work)	Personal Profile System© (PPS)
Documenting personal values, needs, and interests	Guided individual process
Assessment of skills against criteria for mentors	Mentor/PSM© interpretation
Elements of workable agreeements	Presentation
Setting project reporting requirements with program coordinator	Discussion
Feedback Principles and Techniques (Feedback and coaching skills)	Self-study or Workshop
Other skill development needed:	
How to get started (e.g. using PPS©)	Guidelines
Negotiating agreement with protégé	Application
Assist protégé with inventory of qualifications for target jobs	Application
Drafting Individual Development Plans	Application with protégé

Tracking the Health of Relationships. A significant part of the coordination responsibility is monitoring relationships and seeing that they remain healthy and productive. This tracking can be accomplished in a variety of ways. In order to reinforce the flexibility of the program and the responsibility of the protégé for his or her own development, the protégé should report progress primarily to the coordinator. A report need not

Exhibit 12. Sample Outline for Group Orientation of Protégés.

Activity	Process/Resources
Complete biographical data sheet	Individual
Self-assessment of generic career and life skills (if not done as pre-work)	Personal Skills Map© (PSM)
Recognizing human motivation needs	Presentation
Researching mission, values, and culture of organization	Group process
Roles of the four parties in the Facilitated Mentoring Program	Presentation/ discussion
Identifying individual work behavior patterns (if not done as pre-work)	Personal Profile System© (PPS)
Documenting personal values, needs, and interests (Individual Development Plan)	Guided individual process
Managing Personal Growth© (Optional)	Workshop
Finding a mentor and negotiating workable agreements	Presentation
Setting project reporting requirements	Discussion with coordinator
Drafting career goals and job targets	Individual work
Making an inventory of qualifications	Application
Negotiating agreement with mentor	Application
Developing Individual Development Plan	Application with mentor

be detailed and formally documented. It might be as simple as an "all is well" telephone call once per quarter or each month.

In addition, the protégé may send a copy of the individual development goals and action plans to the coordinator every month or two. Progress could be noted along with any difficulties. In the orientation outline shown in Exhibit 14 the protégé reports such progress to the coordinator at six-month intervals.

The coordinator may convene meetings of all or some of the mentors in active relationships on a regular basis, perhaps every other month. The protégés can also meet as a group on the alternate month. When it seems appropriate to reconsider the structure and policies of the program, mentors, protégés, and

Exhibit 13. Sample Outline for Individual Orientation of Participants.

Outcomes	Activity/Resources
The Firm:	Coordinator
Mission, goals, and projected growth	
How the mentoring program supports the mission and goals	Philosophy statement
Policies:	Coordinator
What the mentoring program is and isn't	Structure for the program
Where the present job can lead, career paths	Staff manual
What development activities are available within the Firm	
What educational courses are offered within the Firm	
Resources that are available for external education and development activities	
Time and expense reporting when in mentoring activities	
Mentoring program involvement	
Establishing the mentor relationship:	Coordinator
• Initial match	
• How to get the next one	
Negotiating the agreement:	Coordinator
• Confidentiality	
• Duration of the relationship	
• Suggested format	Agreement format
• Elements of the discussion	Examples provided
• No-fault conclusion	
Development Plan:	Coordinator
• Suggested format	Development Plan
• Setting goals for development	
• Creating action plans	Samples provided
• Reporting progress to mentor, Personnel Administration (6 mo.)	
Examples of mentor activities:	Coordinator
• Meetings with participant for coaching or training	
• Observing participant activities and giving feedback later	
• Recommendations for developmental assignments, training, etc.	
• How the mentor and the engagement supervisor(s) or boss interact	

Exhibit 13. Sample Outline for Individual Orientation of Participants, Cont'd.

Recognition for mentors: Coordinator
    Participants who have a particularly good
    example of a mentor activity relay the
    example to the coordinator for recognition
    of the mentor

Coordinator role: Coordinator
- Matching mentor/participant pairs
- Maintaining matrix of active relationships
- Monitoring progress of development with the participant
- Reporting to Partners on progress of mentoring program
- Resource for counsel on issues
- Conclusion of relationships
- Chairing experience meetings with mentors
- Chairing experience meetings with participants

Source: Rooney, Ida, Nolt and Ahern, 1989. Used with permission.

bosses may meet together for an open discussion of experiences. All these techniques can help to keep relationships healthy and vital.

➤   *The coordinator must see the relationship as an ongoing, changeable organism that is constantly monitored.*

Checklist

As you can see, the task of coordinator must go to a skillful, multitalented person. Use Exhibit 14 to help structure this role.

Exhibit 14. Checklist for Structuring the Role of Coordinators.

	Action to Take
1. Where will we place the coordination function?	

Exhibit 14. Checklist for Structuring the Role of Coordinators, Cont'd.

2. What will the level of the coordinator(s) be?

3. How will we assess the skills of coordinator candidates?

4. What training will be made available to the coordinator(s)?

5. What program-management responsibilities will the coordinator(s) have?

6. What resources will be made available for coordination?

7. Who will be the sounding board for the coordinator?

8. What types of reporting and tracking will we want?

9. _____

10. _____

12

Negotiating Sound Mentoring Agreements

After the mentor and protégé have been matched and have attended orientations, they must negotiate an agreement. The success of the mentoring relationship will be determined to a great extent by the clarity and reasonableness of this agreement. It does not matter whether the agreement is written on a form or on the back of an old envelope, or not written at all. But the discussion must be clear and complete. Most of the issues that surface during mentoring relationships can be prevented with frank discussions at the outset. This chapter provides suggestions for the key components of an agreement and guidelines for putting the agreement together.

In business organizations, the ideal mentoring agreement is devised by the protégé, mentor, coordinator, and natural boss. Each party brings a set of expectations to the negotiating table. Each may also bring some anxieties and fears. The protégé expects to improve skills, gain political savvy, and increase the chances of being promoted. The mentor expects to be respected, renewed, admired, and perhaps to get an extra head and pair of hands to carry out work tasks. The natural boss probably has the least clear expectations, unless the program is a mature one with clearly stated criteria and procedures. The boss who is new to the mentoring process may expect more interference than assistance from the mentor. At a minimum, the agreement must express the outcomes wanted by all three parties. The coordinator is there to see that everyone's interests get served within the goals and objectives of the program.

Basic Guidelines

The articles of indenture of medieval times specified the rights and duties of both the master and the apprentice (Eby and Arrowood, 1940). The master sponsored and cared for the apprentice, and, in turn, the apprentice agreed to guard the master's interests. These agreements went far beyond our current notions of a typical mentor/protégé, employer/employee, or teacher/student relationship. However, two elements need to be specified in any mentoring agreement: the role of the mentor and the goals of the protégé.

Specific Role of the Mentor. The basic nature of the mentoring relationship must be discussed and expressed in the agreement. Some relationships are quite loosely structured — for example, the role of the mentor may be merely to serve as a role model for the protégé or the mentor may be expected simply to invite the protégé to observe the handling of certain activities and events in the usual flow of the mentor's job with time scheduled to discuss the observations and answer questions of the protégé. On the flip side, the mentor may agree to act as an observer when the protégé carries out some tasks or activities. Presumably, time would be scheduled for feedback and perhaps for coaching.

To go a step further on the involvement scale, a mentor may serve as a guide in preparing the protégé for a specific responsibility or task. The mentor may model the desired behaviors, demonstrate, or coach the protégé. The protégé can also be assigned projects that produce a desired result.

When the mentor's role is established ahead of time, both the protégé and mentor have realistic expectations, and the mentor is not tempted to overextend time commitments.

➡️   *Establish the role of the mentor first to focus the agreement.*

Protégé's Goals. The protégé should bring a draft of the development plan to the first meeting with the mentor and coordinator. The plan may have been prepared in collaboration with the boss, it may have been drafted by the protégé alone, or it may have been drafted in the orientation session. It should contain goals and skill areas that the protégé wants to focus on. This document is the foundation of the agreement and determines the type of relationship that ensues.

The negotiated agreement should specify how the development plan will be carried out through mentoring activities. If the mentor and protégé agree to work on only specific skill development, it is relatively easy to describe the activities. It is relatively hard to describe activities for other expectations, such as learning cultural values, making political contacts, and increasing know-how. Unclear or unrealistic expectations are an invitation to disaster for the relationship and perhaps even for the reputation of one or both of the participants. For this reason, expectations need to be expressed in concrete terms. The protégé can say, for example, "My goal is to improve my image in the organization. I'm good at what I do, but my relationship with my co-workers is not great. I want you to help me improve my communication skills." The mentor can then agree to suggest training classes, give honest feedback, or model a successful interaction with others. There is no promise that the protégé will improve, only the promise that the mentor will provide ways for that improvement to happen. After all, a mentor can expose a protégé to the organization's political network through introductions and inside knowledge. But there is no way the mentor can guarantee that the protégé can tap into or be welcome in the political network.

➡ *Tie expectations and goals to skills and specific activities.*

Exhibit 15 provides an example of how to link expectations to specific activities in the negotiated agreement.

Exhibit 15. Sample Worksheet for Individual Development Planning.

Expectations	What Protégé Can Do	What Mentor Can Do
Organizational involvement at higher levels	Presentation to staff	Invite protégé to executive meetings
	Learn more about logistics	Use protégé as resource
Chance to have new ideas heard	Seek opportunities for input	Use protégé as sounding board and act as sounding board for protégé's ideas
		Assignments (projects, task forces)
		Consider opportunities for protégé to contribute
Improve personal style	Be open to feedback	Give protégé honest feedback
	Work to improve weaknesses	Suggest training, role models, etc.

Specific Components

In addition to the two basic components just discussed, a mentoring agreement may include some or all of the following clauses:

Confidentiality Parameters. It is important for the protégé and mentor to trust each other, but both must be comfortable with the kind of information they share. For example, if the protégé confides to the mentor that a co-worker has a drug problem, the mentor may feel obligated to take action. Likewise, the protégé who attends an upper-level meeting may not want the burden of knowing ahead of time which co-workers will be laid off.

It is best to establish at the outset the confidentiality parameters. The mentor might want to say that all information shared by the protégé is confidential; or the mentor might want to hear only information that is pertinent to the development plan. If during the relationship a sensitive issue is discussed and the agreement of confidentiality has been made, it must be honored under reasonable circumstances.

➤ *Discuss how sensitive issues will be handled.*

Duration of Relationship. Agreeing to the approximate duration of the relationship up-front will serve two useful purposes. First, it can be motivating. In fact, setting the conclusion time a little short of what might normally be expected is desirable. A looming date for the conclusion of the formal relationship instills a sense of urgency in both mentor and protégé to make the development activities rigorous. The action plan takes on real meaning when events are scheduled fairly tightly. Second, establishing an ending date also reinforces the temporary nature of the relationship, which helps to prevent dependence and possessive behavior by either party.

The development goals and plans for the protégé should be used to establish the duration of the relationship at the beginning. Progress toward accomplishment of those agreed goals and the wishes of both parties can drive renegotiating the date if appropriate.

➤ *Set a realistic and flexible stopping date.*

No-Fault Termination. The agreement should specify intervals for examining the relationship. At some point, both parties must ask the question, Is it still worth it? If the answer is no, one must have the option of getting out of the agreement.

Deciding how a soured relationship will be concluded before it begins is something like putting together a prenuptial contract. The topic of dissolution may take some of the romance out of the prospective relationship, yet it will reduce the likelihood of bitter disagreements later on. The agreement should specify that either party has the option of discontinuing the relationship for any reason, expressed or not. Either may choose to consult the coordinator on how to terminate the agreement gracefully without finding or acknowledging fault.

➤ *Discuss the no-fault conclusion.*

Frequency and Type of Meetings. "How often will we meet?" This is a reasonable question to ask, and again it depends to a great extent on the development activities planned. When the development involves chairing a task force to study an issue or problem, the mentor and protégé may meet only once or twice over a period of months, unless something goes wrong. If the type of development desired is general and the activities fairly unstructured, meetings may be scheduled once or twice a month, perhaps just for lunch. In contrast, if the mentor is to coach, observe, and give feedback to the protégé for several specific tasks, meetings will be frequent.

The type of meeting is the next decision to tackle. Will it be a face-to-face meeting, talking on the telephone, or corresponding? Any of these types can be effective. Phone calls and facsimile messages take some of the headaches and complications out of meeting if the mentor and protégé are located at a distance from each other.

Lack of availability of the mentor when guidance is wanted or needed can be a great disappointment for the protégé. Yet many protégés are reluctant to demand time from a busy mentor. This issue should be discussed during the negotiation of the agreement. The mentor can make a statement such as, "If I start neglecting you, call me on the carpet for it. It's your responsibility to help me keep this agreement, too." In addition, the coordinator might agree to track the meetings and take action if they are not frequent enough for the protégé's needs.

➤   *Consider the specific activities to be accomplished and ease of contact when establishing meeting times and types.*

Guarantees of Promotion. Some protégés might assume that participating in a mentoring program automatically guarantees their eventual promotions. If there is no guarantee, spell it out in the negotiated agreement. In some programs, a successful candidate can expect promotion. In the Executive Candidate Development Program (U.S. General Accounting Office) the recommendation for promotion to executive level is based on the successful execution of the development plan and the recommendations of the supervisor and mentor. Program participants know these requirements ahead of time and are realistic about what the program can mean to them.

➤   *Clearly state the guarantees, if any.*

Agreement Form

Some organizations require that the mentoring agreement be documented on a standard form. Others require no documentation at all, although for best results, some notes should be made about the agreement and its parameters.

➤   *Prepare suggested agreement forms.*

Exhibit 16 is one type of form that may be used for documenting the negotiated mentoring agreement.

Exhibit 16. Sample Mentoring Agreement Form.

Mentor and Participant Agreement

We are voluntarily entering into a mentoring relationship which we expect to benefit both of us and the Firm. We want this to be a rich, rewarding experience with most of our time together spent in substantive development activities. To minimize the administrative details we have noted these features of our relationship:

- Confidentiality _____
  _____

- Duration of the relationship _____
  _____

- Frequency of meetings _____
  _____

- Approximate amount of time to be invested by mentor _____
  _____

- Specific role of the mentor (model, guide, observe and give
  feedback, recommend developmental activities, facilitate learning,
  suggest/provide resources, etc.) _____
  _____

- Additional points _____
  _____

☐　We have discussed the mentoring experience as a further developmental opportunity and its relationship to the policies and procedures of the Firm.

☐　The skill areas to be the focus of the current development period are noted on the individual development plan maintained by the participant.

☐　We agree to a *no-fault* conclusion of this relationship if, for any reason, it seems appropriate.

_____　　_____
Mentor　　　　　　　　　　　　　　Participant

_____　　_____
Date　　　　　　　　　　　　　　　Date

Source: Rooney, Ida, Nolt and Ahern, 1989. Used with permission.

Checklist

Having a clear agreement saves lots of headaches for everyone involved. It is easier to edit than it is to create, so you will save time for mentors and protégés by giving them suggestions for negotiating their agreements. The checklist in Exhibit 17 gives you an opportunity to prepare for negotiating agreements in your program.

Exhibit 17. Checklist for Negotiating Mentoring Agreements.

	Action to Take
1. What kind of role will mentors be expected to take?	_____
2. How will we deal with issues of confidentiality?	_____
3. Who will be involved in discussing/negotiating the agreement?	_____
4. What duration of the relationship will be suggested, if any?	_____
5. How will development time be reported for the protégé? for the mentor?	_____
6. How can the agreement be concluded, if other than at the specified time?	_____
7. _____	_____
8. _____	_____

13

Evaluating Program Effectiveness

In Part Two of this book, you have been reading about strategies to make a facilitated mentoring program work in your organization. Knowing whether you are getting what you want from these strategies means having some process for tracking and analyzing the results. In Chapter Seven, you examined several techniques to use for determining organizational readiness for a facilitated mentoring program. Some of those same strategies will yield information about what kind of results you want to be able to look at and assess with an evaluation. For example, you may wish to determine the impact of the mentoring experience on the promotion rates of the participants, on their skills acquisition, or on the costs of grooming leaders.

The initial enthusiasm for designing a facilitated mentoring program may obscure the importance of measuring the program's effectiveness. If you think you may want to evaluate the program at some future time, it is best to design the evaluation process as you formulate the components of your program. If you wait to collect opinions and to measure performance until after the program has been initiated, you will have contaminated data. "It [is] important to build performance objectives and a time line for performance, including the acquisition of resources, into the strategy. Resources should include expertise in evaluation" (Hively, 1990). The message is, plan the evaluation at the outset.

Many examples of the importance of evaluation exist in education, especially when the results of evaluations lead to approval of grant proposals. Although the funding for your facilitated mentoring program may not depend on an evaluation of its efficacy, such an evaluation can help to justify the continuation of the program during lean times.

This chapter outlines some basic evaluation concepts and techniques. Strategies that are most relevant to assessing the impact of a mentoring program are described. When you feel inclined to throw up your hands and say, "I don't want to deal with all that! All I want to know is, does this program do anything for my people?", skip to the checklist at the end of the chapter to get an overview of the essential elements of an evaluation.

Key Terms and Concepts

Decision makers are concerned mostly with the value, effectiveness, costs, cost benefits, and cost effectiveness of new programs (Orlansky, 1989). Methods for examining these outcomes have been fairly well established for functions other than human-resource development. It is time the available research on evaluation was applied rigorously to training and development.

Costs. Costs are the resources, expressed in monetary terms, needed by a program to accomplish a desired result. Resources needed for training, for example, include course materials, equipment and facilities, students' and instructors' time. All programs consume resources. Resources assigned to one program are no longer available for other programs. The assignment of funds to a particular program is, in effect, a decision to pursue a particular course of action and not its alternatives.

Costs use common units — that is, money — to measure the various inputs used to produce a specific output — for example, trained people. For better or for worse, determining the costs of programs makes it possible to compare all such programs using a common unit of measurement. This does not imply that it is easy to determine all the resources needed to accomplish a particular training program or that it is easy to obtain the direct costs of all resources. It may be possible to know, for example, only that a mentoring program's strength is that it creates a positive image of the organization.

Effectiveness. The effectiveness of a training program is the extent to which people can do what they were trained to do. It is the output of the resources expended by a training program. Because the purpose of training is to improve performance and, to some extent, turn a novice into an expert, measuring effectiveness requires you to measure the amount of improvement in performance that a particular method of training (including mentoring) produces. Typically, effectiveness is measured by the amount of improvement in performance produced by a new, compared with a previous, method of training.

Problems concerned with collecting effectiveness data generally involve identifying the relevant measures of effectiveness (more than one may be required) and demonstrating that student performance measured in the test environment will, in fact, also occur later in the workplace or operational context. The collection of training performance data that satisfy statistical and analytical requirements is almost always difficult.

Cost Effectiveness. Cost and effectiveness are independent measures of the input and output of a particular training program. A comparison of the cost and effectiveness of alternative methods of training should provide the information a decision maker needs to make an informed choice among the options. For example, if two training programs produce equally effective results, the choice would be the less costly one. Or if two programs cost about the same, the choice should be the more effective one. Specifically the cost-effectiveness methodology fixes the value of either the input or the output. If the input is held constant, we can compare two methods of training that cost about the same and select the one that is more effective. If the output is held constant (for example, attrition is reduced by 20 percent), we can compare two methods of training that are equally effective and select the one that costs less.

It is always possible that some external factor that is not, or cannot be, included in the cost-effectiveness evaluation of training programs will significantly influence the final decision. Sometimes external factors are rational (for example, insufficient funds, changes in the economy, changes in ownership, or a new chief executive officer). Sometimes they are not rational (for example, the outright rejection of mentoring, the nonacceptance of simulations), even though they are clearly cost-effective. In any case, a cost-effectiveness evaluation can provide guidance to a decision maker, but the decision maker must still decide what to do.

Cost-Benefit Analysis. A distinction should be made between a cost-benefit and a cost-effectiveness analysis. A cost-benefit analysis is one in which both the input and output values can be measured in monetary terms. This analysis requires an open market to assess the value (in monetary terms) of the outputs resulting from a particular use of resources (that is, the benefits). One example might be a cost-benefit analysis of a particular form of advertising. The costs are those needed to develop and conduct a particular advertising program; the benefits are the profits that may be attributed to the advertising program.

Cost-effectiveness analysis avoids the limitation of determining monetary values of both inputs and outputs. Clearly, however, if the data are available, a cost-benefit analysis is preferable because both input and output can be compared using the same units.

Value to the Organization. The value of training is the extent to which it contributes to the success of the organization. This type of measurement requires statements as to why the program was initiated in the first place. Was it to increase production, retain personnel, develop personnel, or increase profits? The intent is most likely a combination of desired outcomes. For example, motivation, attitude, and skills development for an employee result in increased productivity and decreased personnel turnover. A facilitated mentoring program typically adds greater value than it costs in that it does not involve out-of-pocket costs nor lost productive time.

Measurement Considerations

Certain measurement considerations must be resolved regardless of the level of analysis (organizational impact or individual performance) or the type of measurement (products, end states, or process consistency of procedures employed).

The value to the organization is the information required to permit either cost-effectiveness or cost-benefit assessment. The measures used to determine whether a program adds value must meet these criteria:

- Validity. Do the measures selected accurately measure what they are intended to measure (for example, attrition, motivation, increased skills)?
- Reliability. How consistently do selected measures yield the same results under similar circumstances (for example, do different raters agree)?
- Generalizability. How comparable are the results of the measures?

The values you decide to measure, the assessment instruments you select, and the approach decided on dictate to a great extent the findings you obtain. If you select attrition as a value, then your data will be attrition statistics. They will not indicate the satisfaction or skills of the protégés. In practice, it is good to select a variety of measures to aid you in your decision process. The simplest approach is to reduce the measures or indices to the cost or monetary value. Then you have a common unit. If possible, invest in more than one approach to increase the soundness of your judgment.

Ultimately the key question is, What information, presented in what format, is sufficient to permit the decision makers to make an informed choice? I discuss now some special considerations for answering this question when we are considering the development process of mentoring.

Special Considerations for Evaluation of Mentoring Programs

Mentoring programs are interactive and nonlinear. In other words, the protégé and the mentor interact, and they, in turn, influence and are influenced by other components of the organization. Further, these interactions and influences occur in a convoluted if not chaotic manner. Therefore, an assessment can rarely isolate a single factor or simply sum up several factors.

What do these facts suggest about how you design your program evaluation? You must not expect a single condition or measure to yield sufficient data for decision making. As has been discussed in previous chapters, the characteristics of both the protégé and the mentor must be considered. In particular, the leadership styles of mentors may well have a different impact with different types of protégés, and these results may vary in different contexts—that is, in a particular type of organization or in an unusual functional department.

An example of the impact of leadership styles in different situations may shed additional light on this concept. A study of U.S. Army platoon performance (H. H. McFann, interview by author, 1990) compared aptitude (intelligence) of platoon members, motivation of platoon members, and leadership style (directive or nondirective) of the platoon leader. None of the factors by itself was significantly related to platoon performance. However, different results were obtained when the leadership style was combined with the other two variables. The nondirective leadership style was found to be most effective with high-aptitude platoons whether they were motivated or not. In contrast, directive leadership was found to be most effective when the platoon members were, on the average, lower in aptitude and were highly motivated. If they were not motivated, then nondirective leadership was most effective.

The message is simple. Straight overall assessments may

not tell you everything you need to know. However, don't be discouraged. Your initial planning for assessment will provide a good start. The following strategies are provided to assist you in undertaking this important and valuable activity.

Developing the Evaluation Plan

What do you want to know about the impact of your mentoring program on the organization? What will you do with the data once you have them? The answers to these questions are key to the evaluation process. If you have no intention of changing the program, don't go through the exercise of putting elaborate data-collection and data-analysis processes in place. If you just want to know how happy it makes people to have the mentoring program, a simple survey will yield this happiness index. If you plan to use the evaluation data to adjust the mentoring program for increased effectiveness, you want to isolate each variable to the extent possible so that you know the impact it has. Or you may want to compare the impact of the facilitated mentoring program with that of other development strategies. In this case some form of comparative analysis is called for. Such an analysis will require collecting data on each of the strategies, the interaction of those strategies, and the impact of both on the results you are analyzing.

Your regular management reports and personnel records may contain most of the data you require to evaluate your mentoring program, particularly if you have a computer database with records of education, training, and work experiences for your employees. Alleman (1982) cites several performance measures that can be compared to determine the long-term impact of mentoring, including number of months in leadership positions on committees and task forces, number of positions of responsibility in community and professional organizations, promotion rates, number of merit-pay raises, turnover rates, productivity rates, and performance ratings.

Where do you start in developing an evaluation plan? At the risk of sounding facetious, I say start where you are. What results are you getting with the training and development processes that you now have in place? These are your baseline indicators. Look particularly at executive development, management training, supervisory training, technical-skills training, climate change or culture change, and ethnic- and gender-sensitivity programs. Look at your projected human-resource requirements, and determine how well you are filling those through current development and recruitment efforts. If no systematic evaluation is being done in development programs, you might go back and look at your readiness assessment from Chapter Seven.

Next, list the results you imagine the mentoring program might have. Do you expect the mentoring program to have a positive effect on

- Recruitment
- Turnover
- Employee skills
- Readiness for higher-level responsibilities
- Flexibility of work force
- Motivation of protégés
- Motivation of mentors
- Current costs of training and development
- Public opinion about your organization

Implementing the Evaluation Plan

Once you have your baseline indicators and an overall idea of the specific results you will be evaluating, you can use the following guidelines to evaluate whether or not your facilitated mentoring program is achieving what you want in these areas.

Protégé Progress. Whether you will include all those who wish to participate or just a target group such as executives, start by setting up a tracking system for the protégé participants. Here are some of the main items to consider tracking:

- Protégé profiles and current assignment
- Skills at beginning of mentoring

- Start dates in the program
- Planned development
- Time spent on development activities
- Costs for development time away from the job, training courses, and other costs
- Reporting to be done

Forms that record both experiences and actions should be completed by both the mentor and the protégé at agreed intervals during the process. Such forms will provide facts, figures, and feelings for evaluation. Some organizations make the coordinator or one of the coordinator's staff the person to gather this data. At General Electric, "a training staff member visits the trainee midway through the seven-month mentoring period, [and] at the one-year mark they're asked how the mentoring relationship worked" (O'Reilly, 1989, p. 4).

Having baseline data is important. If you do some type of developmental diagnosis in preparation for the protégé's development plan, you have a baseline for measuring increased promotability when the mentoring relationship is officially concluded. The protégé can complete the same assessment instruments again to get a before and after look at the data. Or you may ask both mentor and boss to rate the degree of change in the protégé's skills as well as the promotability of the protégé. Phillips-Jones (1983) suggests keeping track of protégés once they leave the program and plotting their progress on their career paths.

➡ *Install a system to track the career progress of the protégés.*

Mentor Experience. You will also want baseline data on the mentors in your program. A simple questionnaire will do. Some typical questions might be: "How do you rate the usefulness of such a program?" "Do you see yourself having the knowledge and skills to be a successful mentor?" "Are the program requirements clear and concise?" Other subjects that might be covered are:

- Knowledge and skills of the mentor relevant to selection criteria

- Mentor attitudes toward the organization and loyalty to it
- Career plans
- Expectations for the mentoring relationship
- Time invested
- Perception of mentor's responsibilities
- Discrepancies between what mentors are expected to do and what they are doing

Similar responses and reactions can be gathered periodically during the mentoring process and at the conclusion of each relationship. Unusual situations reported in survey questionnaires can be clarified with follow-up telephone or in-person interviews by the coordinator. Comparison of the data from each point in the relationship will give you a picture of trends in the opinions of the mentors during the process.

This type of evaluation is used in 3M's New Employee Mentor Program. Each mentor and mentee (protégé), in addition to the mentee's supervisor, completes an assessment questionnaire on the program following the six-month assignment. "This feedback provides a basis for continual refinement of the program to meet the needs of the new hires, their supervisors and the engineering organization" (Leschke, 1984, p. 13).

Don't think that every mentor assessment you do must be long and scientific. In fact, the easier an evaluation is, the more likely you are to get cooperation. Merrill Lynch (Phillips-Jones, 1983) encourages mentors to drop short, one-paragraph memos to the coordinator highlighting activities they have shared with their protégés.

➤ *Find a way to track the mentor's attitudes.*

Turnover Rate in Target Group. Reduced turnover among the protégés is an oft-cited benefit of mentoring. To test this conclusion, you must know the rate of turnover across the organization and for the target group prior to implementing the mentoring program. Tracking the rate of turnover for the target group is the easy part. Keep in mind that you must also analyze the reasons for the turnover. For example, a skillful mentor may help someone who is inappropriate for a job make the decision to leave that job. Isolating all the other variables that may have a causal relationship with turnover is difficult. At the least you will want to know how your turnover statistics compare with those of other organizations in similar industries or professions, both before and after the implementation of your facilitated mentoring program.

In addition to looking at the numbers or percentages, you must be aware of the monetary costs of turnover to the organization. Are people lost from critical jobs where a vacancy means lost productivity or failure to provide an essential service to a client? What is the cost of replacement, including the recruiting, hiring, orientation, and perhaps training of new people? These baseline data, when considered with all the other variables, will help you make an accurate assessment of the cost effectiveness of the facilitated mentoring program.

→   *Capture statistics on turnover in the total organization, in the target group, and in other similar organizations before you start.*

Costs of Training and Development. If you have baseline data on the current costs of training and development programs, then, by assessing the same costs after facilitated mentoring has been in place for a while, you can judge whether there is a cost reduction.

Calculating the costs of training is a challenge for everyone, even those with the most automated accounting systems. However, personnel database software is becoming comprehensive and reasonable in cost. Only a few years ago, the only computer programs for personnel data ran on large mainframes with software costs running into five figures. Installation and data entry increased the costs significantly. Now human-resource software for micros and personal computers costs just a few hundred dollars. It can be installed with relational databases providing fifty or more standard reports, including skills inventories and skills searches.

To capture the cost of training, begin by looking at the amount of time trainees spend away from the job while in

formal training courses, a cost that is often obscured. The registration fees for external programs are even more difficult to
isolate. These fees might be considered an education cost, a
tuition cost, or a travel cost. Related expenses for travel, accom-
modations, and incidentals may be reported as the cost of
training, or they may be taken from a separate pocket in the
budget.

➤ *Calculate the costs associated with all the elements of training.*

Cost of Administration. The cost of staffing the coordinator
position or positions is easy to track. Other administrative costs
may be subsumed in the cost of maintaining the personnel
department. It may be more trouble than it is worth to your
organization to try to isolate such costs; however, a complete
evaluation would include all available data.

➤ *Establish a database for recording administrative costs of the
mentoring program.*

Other Items. The duration of the relationships can be
tracked by keeping records of mentor/protégé pairs, the dates
the mentoring agreements were negotiated, and the dates they
were concluded.

In order to prevent obstacles in the program, record the
issues reported by mentors and protégés. These comments can
be invited in the interviews done with individuals or in the
experience meetings conducted with groups of mentors and
protégés.

➤ *Set up a simple reporting process for both mentors and protégés
at regular intervals.*

Checklist

Now you must decide how extensive you wish your evaluation to be. When you have the basic evaluation outcomes in

mind, go on to the checklist in Exhibit 18 to make notes on how to collect pertinent data.

Exhibit 18. Checklist for Designing an Evaluation of the Program.

Action to Take

1. Why did we start this program in the first place? _____

2. What do we want the mentoring program to do for our organization? _____

3. How do we define success for the mentoring program? _____

4. What will we do with the results of the evaluation? _____

5. What data must we have to make decisions about the future of the program? _____

6. How can we get the data we need? _____

7. What reporting will be required/ requested of
   • mentors?
   • protégés?
   • the coordinator? _____

8. What is our database capability now? _____

9. _____

14

Gender, Culture,
and Relationship Concerns

Until now, this book has focused primarily on the practical aspects of putting facilitated mentoring programs together. This chapter deals with specific concerns that people have about the mentoring relationship: gender issues, sexual attractions, cross-cultural pairing, racism, and a potpourri of other problems that can occur when two people are brought together.

Gender Issues

The spontaneous attraction between two people can stimulate positive energy for both and result in increased productivity for the organization. An arranged match may miss that spontaneous surge of excitement yet still be productive by all measures. To make arranged matches work the organization can identify multiple candidates for the mentor role and allow the protégé to spend time with each to see how the chemistry develops. Avoiding a serious mismatch is the responsibility primarily of the coordinator. The match must not be forced if either of the pair does not like or respect the other. Allowing the protégé to nominate several mentor candidates and providing some tools for assessing skills, behaviors, and interests will go a long way toward increasing the likelihood of compatible work behaviors and personalities. However, most of the literature on mentoring (Collins, 1983; Driscoll and Bova, 1980; Clawson and

173

Kram, 1984) has dealt with the other extreme: avoiding the relationship that becomes too personal and emotional.

Like any close involvement, the relationship between the mentor and protégé has the potential to become personal and emotionally charged. The pair may discuss the potential for personal involvement, agree to maintain objectivity in the relationship, and then find it impossible to maintain the desired emotional or physical distance.

Even when there is no romantic interest between a protégé and mentor, gossips will often manufacture it. Mary Cassatt and Edgar Degas had a long-standing professional relationship—nearly forty years—and though both denied ever being lovers, rumors abounded (McMullen, 1984). More recently the notorious relationship between Bill Agee and Mary Cunningham at Bendix (Liles, 1989) was given lots of press through all the stages of their working together, while they denied that there was any intimate involvement, and the interest in their relationship continues even now that they are married to each other.

Why do many people think that professional women, especially those who have fought long and hard for a promotion, would risk their careers for a romantic relationship with a mentor? The proliferation of special programs for women perpetuates the assumption that women do not know how to behave in the workplace. They are different (read *deficient*) and therefore require remedial training. Look at the titles of the seminars and workshops marketed to women: "Assertiveness Training for Women" (CareerTrack, 1990), "Image and Communication Skills for Women" (National Businesswomen's Leadership Association, 1990), "What Makes the Difference: Success Strategies for the Promotable Woman" (Management Training Systems, 1990), and on and on. Perhaps these seminars are popular because people believe that women inherently do not have the right psychological makeup for managerial roles. In a survey of training programs for women and men, Berryman-Fink and Fink (1985) found that organizational structures and management theories have traditionally been derived from the military and team sports, predominantly male spheres of influence.

Compared with these macho models, the female seems to be a misfit and in need of special training. However, the role of mentor more often involves one-on-one activities than team plays.

Research suggests, however, that most women and men do not abandon all sense of propriety when they become mentor and protégé. A study of spontaneous mentoring relationships by Alleman (1982) suggested that mentoring behavior does not vary with differences in the sex of mentors or protégé or with the gender mix in the pairs. In the study, Alleman included personality characteristics, taking into consideration actual and perceived characteristics.

Because of these prevailing beliefs, and in spite of some evidence to the contrary, cross-gender pairings will continue to be a subject of special concern. One issue is the structure of the relationship itself. A common stereotype of the mentoring dyad is that the mentor will be male and the protégé a younger male. In fact, women who are seeking a mentor at a higher level will still have to choose mostly from men.

Sexual attraction does occur in some mentor/protégé relationships. We all know people who have had sexual affairs with co-workers or bosses. Personal involvement with others is a fact of working life. Whether these relationships are harmful or helpful is open to debate. "Sexual attraction can't be stopped and it can enhance the organization. It should be managed so it has a positive, not negative, effect on the organization and its people," says organization development consultant Kaleel Jamison (quoted in Spruell, 1985, p. 21). However, Harrigan (1977, p. 287) says this will always be a no-win situation for women. "Business sex is guided and directed by a set of conscious and unconscious rules that are invariably beneficial to men and deleterious to women who work in the same corporate institution. *Women can't win this game*. They must not play . . . if they want to remain viable activists in the impersonal master game of corporate politics where the goal is money, success, and independent power."

To avoid the dangers of a sexual attraction in a male mentor/female protégé relationship, the pair often opt for a father/daughter form of behavior. According to Kram (1985, pp. 22–23), both careers will suffer from this adaptation. "The woman who colludes in playing a helpless and dependent role forfeits the opportunity to demonstrate her skills and competence. The male mentor who maintains the role of tough, invulnerable expert forfeits the opportunity to ask for help when it would be useful."

Managers and administrators have traditionally tried to ignore office affairs, hoping they will not be noticed or will go away. More seriously, they often also ignore reported instances of sexual harassment because they do not want to deal with this hot potato and often because they believe it can be expected. Fury (1980, p. 46), commenting on the implied contract of sexual favors in return for male sponsorship, says, "I wouldn't say there's always an erotic aspect to such relationships, but it's there quite often. . . . How many times to bed equals one promotion?"

Suggestions on how to deal with the sexual attraction of people in the same office rather than ignore it have ranged from referral for counseling to ousting one or both of those involved. Most of the time, the woman loses her job. But perhaps we should not overlook the powerful energy exuded by people in love or in other emotional involvements. Einstein is reputed to have accomplished most of his creative work in three spurts—each of the three times he was madly in love!

Here are some guidelines that can be included in the orientation for mentors and protégés for handling the issues of personal attraction:

- Acknowledge the potential for sexual attraction, particularly in the closeness of a mentoring relationship.
- Discuss the organization's policy on sexual harassment, homosexuality, dating other employees, employment of related persons, and other related concerns.
- Identify the negative and destructive as well as the positive aspects of sexual tensions on the job.
- Specify the types of relationships that are absolutely taboo—for example, between co-workers reporting to the

same supervisor, when one of the pair is reporting to the other, or when one or both are married.

- Describe the consequences of violations of policy and/or taboos.
- Establish the recourses available when either one has behaved inappropriately in the relationship.

Another gender issue in mentoring is the belief that upper-level women do not help their female co-workers advance. This myth can be dispelled. Consider this quote from one of Bowen's (1985, p. 33) study respondents in a female/female dyad, "I now move in an entirely different circle. I have even changed who I want to be. An enormous impact! She makes sure I meet people." Bowen's study, limited to fourteen female mentor/ female protégé pairs and eleven male mentor/female protégé pairs, clearly showed that it is not the gender of the mentor but the functions provided by the mentor that account for whether the protégé sees her career as on the fast track or not. Those functions involve using many characteristics traditionally described as feminine: caring, nurturing, and protecting.

In fact, evidence indicates that women may make better mentors for both male and female protégés. Internationally renowned anthropologist Ashley Montagu (1974) describes women's interpersonal skills as superior to those of men. "The female's practice of the art of human relations continues throughout life; and this is one of the additional reasons that enable women to perceive the nuances and pick up the subliminal signs in human behavior which men usually fail to perceive" (p. 182).

Josefowitz (1982) reported a study focused on the accessibility of managers to their subordinates that yielded some surprising results: Women managers were found to be twice as accessible to their employees as men managers, regardless of their positions. This statistic would suggest that women may have the edge as mentors because they will be more readily available than men to interact with their protégés.

Cross-Cultural Issues

It always seems easier to make contact with and relate to people who are just like ourselves than to those who are not. In most U.S. businesses and in the government the majority of senior managers and administrators are still white males. In this situation the biggest problem with informal mentoring for the minority protégé is finding someone to develop a relationship with. Interacting with people who look different or behave differently takes more energy than some people want to give to a situation. As one protégé in a budding mentor relationship puts it (Wilkens, 1989, p. 6), "It's not that people are prejudiced, it's just that they don't share a common experience. A white male is more likely to relate to another white male than to a Hispanic male like me. With someone from my own background, I don't have to explain where I'm coming from." (However, mentors can also be intolerant and judgmental of those who resemble themselves, especially if their protégés make the same mistakes they did [Flaxman, 1990].)

In the work environments of the future, there will be little choice about working with one group of people rather than another. The work force is increasingly diverse. AT&T projects that 82 percent of new employees will be women, minorities, and immigrants (Montana, 1988). Obviously, people must learn to live and work successfully with others of widely varying cultural backgrounds and needs.

This increasing diversity is all the more reason for facilitating the mentoring process because the organization can then deliberately pair mentors and protégés from different ethnic or cultural backgrounds. Such pairs will have some unusual demands made on them. Preparing the parties for successful cross-cultural relationships will be a challenge for the coordinator.

In the early 1980s many workshops and seminars on sensitivity training were made available to those working with minorities, blacks in particular. Obviously, organizations cannot continue to invent training programs to teach people to deal with every ethnic group in the country. But people can study the culture of those with whom they work and pay particular attention to the similarities and differences of individuals.

Understanding a different group does not mean expecting less of them, however. George E. Curry, New York bureau chief of the *Chicago Tribune*, does not believe in the special treatment of minorities (interview by author, 1990). Curry, who has mentored numerous young people interested in journalism, states, "Some nonminorities have confided to me that, deep down, they have some reluctance about being 'too hard' on African-Americans and other minority group members for fear of being labeled a racist. I think it's racist *not* to challenge minority students."

How can mentoring help to improve cultural exchanges in organizations? Acquisitions of American companies by Japanese firms have brought the issue of different cultural styles into sharp focus. American workers, who have operated under authoritarian managers, do not understand and respond to the team approach. A mentor who has experience with the opposite culture can help to accelerate the learning process. In many of these cases, combining functions such as payroll handling or personnel means that many experienced staff people at high levels are declared redundant. These people can be designated as mentors to teach new employees the ins and outs of the different culture (Zey, 1988).

What can a mentor do when the issue of racism in the organization comes up? Confront it and deal with it honestly. Curry (1990, p. 11), who works primarily with students, states, "If one is to have a meaningful relationship with a student, minority or otherwise, then one has to be honest, especially about the prevalence of racism. The minority student who hears from a mentor that racism no longer exists might question that mentor's candor. On the other hand, one can say, 'Yes, there is indeed racism in the United States and it is not likely to go away in your lifetime.' Having said that, it is important to then add, 'You can beat the odds. You can become successful in spite of racism or discrimination.'"

Other Problems for the Mentoring Pair

As in all relationships, many complications and problems can come up. In previous chapters I suggested strategies for preventing and remedying sticky relationship issues: periodic feedback to the coordinator, a no-fault conclusion, and a de-tailed, realistic agreement. These and other strategies can be used to deal with the most common relationship complaints.

Perception That Needs Are Not Met. As we have suggested, unrealistic expectations for the outcomes of the mentoring rela-tionship can lead to growing hostility between the parties. But even when the mentor and protégé have discussed and agreed to specific outcomes and the relationship is amicable, the protégé can feel that his or her needs are not being met. With the contact and proximity, the mentor is an easy target and may be blamed for shortcomings that are, in fact, the protégé's. The mentor can suggest that the protégé write out expectations (see Exhibit 15 as a sample) and ideas for how they can be met as a start for resolving this concern.

Mentor Too Possessive. Feeling trapped by a possessive mentor who won't let go is a common complaint of protégés. Some are strong enough to negotiate themselves out of the relationship with no damage done to either participant. Others just drift along without initiating contact with the mentor, hop-ing the relationship will die a natural death. When all else fails, the coordinator may have to intervene to convince the mentor to let go. Not all mentors are possessive, of course. One mentor told me that one of the most rewarding experiences of his life was seeing a former protégé promoted to a level above himself (T. Swift, interview by author, 1989).

Personality Clashes. When mentors are assigned rather than mutually selected, it is easy for behaviors and styles to clash. Making participation entirely voluntary, providing multiple mentors, and giving the pair an opportunity for a get-acquainted period prior to negotiating the development agreement can decrease the likelihood that a match will be made between people with completely different personalities.

Protégé Too Ambitious. When the protégé is too close for comfort (organizationally speaking), the mentor may be reluctant to assist with further development. "Why develop my own competition?" The ambitions of the protégé can also become an obstacle if they cause unnecessarily aggressive behaviors. For example, a protégé who wants to appear in the know might make public information shared in confidence by the mentor.

The coordinator may be asked to intervene if other career guidance might be useful. Skip-level mentors are less likely to feel threatened. The boss and mentor can collaborate on how to counsel a protégé on the realism of ambitions. Similarly, they can provide counsel on the consequences of violating confidences.

Some popular literature suggests that these problems do not occur in happenstance, informal mentoring relationships. That claim is not only romantic but doubtful. All relationships have their problems. By being aware of potential problems and dealing with them head on when they occur, an organization can have a facilitated mentoring program that is successful and long-lived.

Jealousy, Favoritism, Skepticism, Cloning, and Other Conflicts

In Chapters Eight and Nine, guidelines were given for selecting and preparing mentors and protégés for their roles in an effective mentoring relationship. Many of the issues that may arise between these two primary parties were discussed there, along with strategies for preventing serious problems. This section examines some other management and organizational issues and describes preventive actions for those.

Jealousy. When the mentoring program is not clearly and openly publicized throughout the organization, it can provoke some emotional reactions from those who are not involved.

Some protégés in informal relationships have felt that a facilitated mentoring program would have lessened the amount of jealousy they experienced when others suspected they were getting special treatment from a mentor (P. Schaub, interview by author, 1990.)

Even when programs are openly publicized, those people who are not participants may be jealous of the protégés. "Fast-trackers," "fair-haired boys," and "jet jobs" are labels attached to those who are known to be considered promotable, especially when they are engaged in special development activities. Your best strategy to keep this symptom from jeopardizing the program is to make the program parameters and selection criteria clear. Explain to nonparticipants how they can become involved and stress the choices they have.

Also, the direct subordinates of a mentor may be jealous of their boss's spending time with a protégé. Mentors may be suspected of neglecting their own employees when their protégés are outside the unit. This suspicion may be unfounded. When asked what effects, if any, participation in the mentoring relationship had on relationships with other subordinates, one executive at Federal Express replied, "I'm not taking time away from anyone in my organization" (quoted in Avant and Crosby DeBerry, 1985).

Perception of Favoritism. Labor unions or other groups who represent employees may object to the targeting of specific individuals for future managerial positions. A good strategy for heading off interference is to invite employee representatives to participate in designing the criteria and procedures for the program.

It appears that some unions are now taking a positive view of training and development opportunities offered to employees. In one manufacturing plant where I was a consultant the union pushed for a mentoring program for women to get them beyond the first-line-supervisor jobs. In General Motors plants (Furman, 1990) dislocated workers are offered one-on-one coaching and counseling on career opportunities, and funded training in basic skills, technical skills, and personal skills. Their union, the United Automobile Workers, is said to be strongly supportive of these training and development programs for the people they represent.

Skepticism. When members of an organization are not engaged in development activities for themselves, they tend to be skeptical of the value of all human-resource activities. "I don't need/want/get special training, so why are we spending money on development programs such as mentoring? It ought to be going for newer equipment. What is the bang we're getting for the bucks we're spending on this program?" This kind of concern is a driver for a sound evaluation plan, which was discussed in Chapter Thirteen.

Fear of Cloning. The fear that everyone will look alike, think alike, and behave in similar ways when they are being mentored by a few top managers can create resistance to formalizing the process. The stage play and film *How to Succeed in Business Without Really Trying* carried this point to its extreme by presenting the ludicrous picture of executives literally lockstepping through the office. Many an organization has projected a corporate identity through the apparel of the executives. The school tie is still worn by many European executives. And what corporate logo is called to mind when you see a man in a dark suit, white shirt, and striped tie?

It used to be said that a powerful person (assumed to be male) looks at a potential protégé and sees a younger version of himself. But, as Kanter (1977, p. 184) says, "Who can look at a woman and see themselves?" With an increasingly diverse work force, gender and ethnicity are strong factors that will negatively influence the tendency toward cloning.

A research study conducted by Alleman (1982) found that mentors and their protégés in her experimental group were no more alike in either personality or background than the pairs in her control group of nonmentors and their subordinates. Mentors did not select the same adjectives (from a list of 300) to describe themselves and their protégés any more often than nonmentors in the control group did. However, protégés did describe themselves and their mentors using the same terms. Apparently the protégés perceived a similarity to their mentors that either did not exist or was not perceived by the mentors.

      Conflicts with Other Development Programs. When mentoring is set up as a separate, special program, it has to compete with other development programs for all types of resources. The sooner the program is integrated with other development programs, the less likely this conflict is to occur.

Checklist

      When you review and make your notes on the checklist in Exhibit 19, you will have preventive actions for dealing with the potential obstacles of gender, culture, and other relationship and organizational issues that may occur in your facilitated mentoring program.

Exhibit 19. Checklist for Identifying Gender, Culture, and Relationship Concerns.

	Action to Take
1. What guidelines will be given for cross-gender relationships?	_____
2. How will we prepare mentors and protégés who are from different races or cultures?	_____
3. What measures can be taken to ensure that the protégé's needs are being met?	_____
4. How can we minimize personality clashes?	_____
5. What can be done to avoid the mentor's possessiveness from getting in the way of being a good mentor?	_____
6. When criticism of the program arises because of relationship problems, what tactic will we take?	_____

Exhibit 19. Checklist for Identifying Gender, Culture, and Relationship Concerns, Cont'd.

7. What will we do to minimize subordinate jealousy?   _____

8. How will we publicize the program to nonparticipants?   _____

9. How will we collaborate with labor unions or other employee representatives?   _____

10. What will we do to prove the worth of development?   _____

11. What can be done to avoid cloning?   _____

12. What other conflicts do we anticipate, and what can we do to avoid having these jeopardize our program?   _____

13. _____   _____

14. _____   _____

15. _____   _____

15

Making Facilitated Mentoring Work

An article entitled "Take My Mentor, Please," by Peter Kizilos, appeared in the April 1990 issue of *Training Magazine*. This well-written article contained some horror stories about formal mentoring programs: mentors and protégés haphazardly thrown into relationships and left to manage on their own; mentors and protégés not speaking to each other; mentors sabotaging their protégés' careers. According to the article, many organizations use mentoring only as a quick fix. They do not have the culture or the internal support to make such a program successful over the long haul.

The article did, however, have a few positive things to say about formal mentoring. It cited a successful program in the Internal Revenue District Office in Kansas City, Missouri. People interviewed linked its success to some interesting features of the program:

- The organizational climate already encouraged professional and personal growth.
- Mentors volunteer for the role and receive formal training before entering the relationship.
- A career adviser studies protégés, mentors, their work styles, and their personalities before recommending a match. If the protégé or mentor doesn't think the match is right, it is not forced.

- The relationships are cross-functional, which helps build trust and encourages confidentiality.

Each of these features will sound familiar if you have read most of the chapters in this book.

Facilitated mentoring is not a new idea in Western society. It has been around since ancient Greece, perhaps since the beginning of humanity. Currently, it is being used in many schools and charitable organizations to supplement resources and bring care and nurturing to those who need it. It is a fast-growing trend that is enjoying great success in these areas.

Some argue, however, that businesses in the United States emphasize individual effort too much for mentoring to work; people believe in getting to the top without help. We do not have the patience of the Japanese nor the true team spirit of the Scandinavians. The assumption is that greed and self-serving motives are rampant in American corporations. Meanwhile, divorce statistics in the United States prove that we are becoming worse at managing relationships. The question is, If we can't make a relationship work at home, how can we make one work in our business lives?

Some seasoned managers are optimistic that we can change the typical reactive behavior of U.S. business leaders. To do so we must develop the patience and persistence to see programs that encourage change in organizational structure and in behavior fully implemented and the ensuing benefits realized. Only with persistence will we reap the potential good results of concepts such as total quality, self-managed work teams, and facilitated mentoring.

In reality, some organizations and some people will never be ready for mentoring. Facilitated mentoring programs won't work for everyone. But in the course of writing this book we heard far too many success stories to believe that facilitated mentoring will go the way of the trendy workshops and power suits. Both formal and informal mentoring have helped to create some outstanding administrators, managers, writers, artists, educators, and citizens.

If you believe your organization is ready for facilitated

mentoring, prepare a careful design. Your entries on the check-lists at the end of each of the chapters in Part Two give you the data you must have to construct your plan. Here is a checklist of the most important points to consider in your advance planning:

- Ask yourself why a mentoring program is needed; what is the gap that such a process will fill.
- State the desired outcomes for the program in specific, measurable terms. Specify benefits expected for the organization, mentors, and protégés.
- Assess the readiness of your organization to invest in a long-term program for facilitating mentoring. Is there support from the top and throughout the organization for the two to three years necessary to permit full integration and evaluation?
- Develop an evaluation plan to measure the impact of mentoring on the organization, the mentors, and the protégés.
- Determine where you will place the mentoring function in the organization for administration and reporting.
- Select and train the coordinator(s).
- Prepare a promotional plan; then develop the materials to publicize the program.
- Design the structure and operating procedures for the program. Mentor and protégé identification, selection, orientation, and reporting strategies are the core components of these procedures. Be flexible in your approach.
- Execute the pilot program, gathering data to evaluate and revise as indicated.
- Use your evaluations positively and realistically to make necessary adjustments to the program design.

The mentoring program must grow and change with the priorities and the people needs in the organization. You can even give it a rest for a year or two if your succession needs seem well met.

One final request. When you have some data on your experiences with facilitating the mentoring process in your organization, write them up and get them published! Your success story can save someone else time, effort, and money. Reinventing wheels is not a good use of our time. Every day will bring us new challenges in the development of people. Our combined knowledge and experiences can assure healthy work environments and happy, productive people.

Resource:
Sources of Instruments
for Assessing Growth
and Development

ACUMEN: Insight for Managers (human synergistics®)
ACUMEN, International
3950 Civic Center Drive, Suite 310 North
San Rafael, CA 94903

Managing Personal Growth©
Blessing/White, Inc.
900 State Road
Princeton, NJ 08540

Personal Profile System©
Performax Systems International (Carlson Learning Company)
12755 State Highway 55
Minneapolis, MN 55441

Personal Skills Map©
Dr. Darwin Nelson and Dr. Gary Low
Life Skills Center
5934 South Staples #206
Corpus Christi, TX 78413

SKILLSCOPE©
Center for Creative Leadership
P.O. Box P-1
Greensboro, NC 27402

Or contact MMHA The Managers' Mentors, Inc.
2317 Mastlands Drive, Suite A
Oakland, CA 94611

References

Alleman, E. J. "Getting a Handle on Mentoring—It Can Be Measured and Managed." Unpublished manuscript, Mentor, Ohio, 1982.

American Society for Training and Development. "Benefits of Mentoring." *ASTD Info-Line Series*, Sept. 1986, p. 2.

Andrew, B., and Winchell, M. "A New Workforce: Why Industry Must Understand Changing Demographics." In *Conference Proceedings of The Nation's Workforce: Year 2000*. Milwaukee: University of Wisconsin, 1988.

Anonymous. "A Collaborative Student . . . with Caveats." Unpublished manuscript, Vancouver, B.C., Canada, Dec. 3, 1989.

Appel, M., and Trail, T. "Building Effective Professional Adult Education Mentoring Relationships." In *Proceedings of the First International Conference on Mentoring*. Vol. 1. Vancouver, B.C.: International Association for Mentoring, 1986.

"Assertiveness Training for Women." *CareerTrack*, 1990.

Avant, L., and Crosby DeBerry, L. "Survey to Evaluate the FEC Mentoring Program." Unpublished survey and videotape, Federal Express Corporation, Memphis, Tenn., 1985.

Avant, L., and Crosby DeBerry, L. "Federal Express Mentoring Survey Summary." Unpublished manuscript, Memphis, Tenn., 1986.

Bandura, A. *Social Foundations of Thought and Action*. Englewood Cliffs, N.J.: Prentice-Hall, 1986.

Beer, M. *Organizational Change and Development: A System View*. Santa Monica, Calif.: Goodyear, 1980.

Bennis, W., and Nanus, B. *Leaders*. New York: Harper & Row, 1985.

Berryman-Fink, C., and Fink, C. R. "Optimal Training for Opposite-Sex Managers." *Training and Development Journal*, 1985, *39*, 26–29.

Blotnick, S. *The Corporate Steeplechase: Predictable Crisis in Business Career*. New York: Facts on File, 1984.

Bowen, D. D. "Were Men Meant to Mentor Women?" *Training and Development Journal*, 1985, *39*, 31–32.

Carmichael, J. M. "Demographic Impact on the Federal Employer." In *Conference Proceedings of The Nation's Workforce: Year 2000*. Milwaukee: University of Wisconsin, 1988.

Cavazos, L. F. "Cavazos Supports Mentoring Programs." In *A Special Report on Mentoring*. Pittsburgh, Pa.: PLUS and The National Education Association, 1990.

Clawson, J. G., and Kram, K. E. "Managing Cross-Gender Mentoring." *Business Horizons*, 1984, *27*, 22–32.

Collins, E.G.C. "Managers and Lovers." *Harvard Business Review*, 1983, *61*, 149–152.

Collins, E.G.C., and Scott, P. "Everyone Who Makes It Has a Mentor." *Harvard Business Review*, 1978, *56*, 217.

Crosby, L. "How to Bring Mentor and Protege Together—Formally." In *Report 1564, Sec. 1: Bureau of Business Practice*. Waterford, Conn.: National Foremen's Institute, 1984.

Crosby, L. "Mentoring at Work in Federal Express Corporation." *The Manager's Mentor*, 1987, *1* (2), 4.

Curry, G. E. "Aim High." In *The Power of Mentoring*. New York: One PLUS One, 1990.

Darling, L.A.W. "Endings in Mentor Relationships." *The Journal of Nursing Administration*, 1985, *15* (11), 40–41.

Davis, J. "Management Development in Banking/Special Problems for Women." *Performance & Instruction*, 1981, *20* (3), 8–14.

Dinnocenzo, D. A. "Labor-Management Cooperation: Keys to Success." In *Conference Proceedings of The Nation's Workforce: Year 2000*. Milwaukee: University of Wisconsin, 1988.

Dole, E. "State of the Workforce." A speech given to the American Society for Training and Development, Orlando, Fla., May 1990.

Driscoll, J. B., and Bova, R. A. "The Sexual Side of Enterprise, Management Review 52." *Training and Development Journal*, 1980, *34*, 21–23.

Eby, F., and Arrowood, C. G. *The History and Philosophy of Education: Ancient and Medieval.* Englewood Cliffs, N.J.: Prentice Hall, 1940.

Everitt, S., and Murray-Hicks, M. "Models, Mentors, and Sponsors for Managers." Presented at the National Society for Performance and Instruction Conference, Montreal, Canada, 1981.

Fagan, M. M. "Do Formal Mentoring Programs Really Mentor?" In *Proceedings of the First International Conference on Mentoring.* Vol. 2. Vancouver, B.C.: International Association for Mentoring, 1986.

Fagan, M. M. "Formal Mentoring in Law Enforcement: An Analysis of the Typical FTO Program." *Mentoring International*, 1989, *3* (2), 17–19.

Fagan, M., and Walter, G. "Mentoring Among Teachers." *The Journal of Educational Research*, 1982, *2*, 113–118.

Farren, C., Gray, J. D., and Kaye, B. *Mentoring: A Boon to Career Development Personnel.* New York: American Management Association, 1984.

Flaxman, E. "Good Mentoring." In *The Power of Mentoring.* New York: One PLUS One, 1990.

Fury, K. "Mentor Mania." *Savvy*, April 1980, pp. 42–47.

Glazer, R. R., and Murray, M. "Mentors — Myth, Magic or Manageable Development Model?" Paper presented at Best of America Conference, New York, January 1990.

Gray, W. A. "Components for Developing a Successful Formalized Mentoring Program in Business, the Professions, Education, and Other Settings." In *Proceedings of the First International Conference on Mentoring.* Vol. 2. Vancouver, B.C.: International Association for Mentoring, 1986.

Gray, W. A. "Situational Mentoring: Custom Designing Planned

Mentoring Programs." *Mentoring International*, 1989, *3* (1), 19–28.

Groder, M. G. "Everything You Want to Know About Mentors (Condensed)." *Boardroom Reports*, 1980, *10*, 5.

Halatin, T. J. *Why Be a Mentor? Part 3*. Minneapolis, Minn.: 3M, 1989.

Harrigan, B. L. *Games Mother Never Taught You*. New York: Rawson Associates, 1977.

Harriman, A. *Women/Men Management*. New York: Praeger, 1985.

Havemann, J. "Management Training: A Mixed Bag in Quality and Relevance." *The Washington Post*. Aug. 12, 1987, p. 21a.

Head, F., and Gray, M. M. "The Legacy of Mentor: Insights into Western History, Literature and the Media." *International Journal of Mentoring*, 1988, *2* (2), 26–33.

Hennig, M., and Jardim, A. *The Managerial Woman*. Garden City, N.Y.: Anchor Doubleday, 1977.

Hively, J. *Ten Steps to a Mentoring Network*. Pittsburgh, Pa.: PLUS, 1990.

Hogan, B. "How to Be a Mentor." *Kiwanis Magazine*, 1984, *69*, 25–28, 47.

Hughes, B. "The Corporate Mentor." *Republic Scene*, Oct. 1980, pp. 50–57.

Image and Communication Skills for Women. Shawnee Mission, Kans.: National Businesswomen's Leadership Association, 1990.

Josefowitz, N. "Women Executives: The Accessibility Factor." *Ms.*, 1989, *10* (8), 89.

Kanter, R. M. *Men & Women of the Corporation*. New York: Basic Books, 1977.

Kirby, P. "The Trinity College Mentor Program." Unpublished manuscript, Trinity College, Washington, D.C., 1989.

Kizilos, P. "Take My Mentor, Please!" *Training*, 1990, *27* (165), 49–55.

Kram, K. E. *Mentoring at Work*. Glenview, Ill.: Scott, Foresman, 1985.

Kram, K. E. *Info-Line—Design Productive Mentoring Programs*. Alexandria, Va.: American Society for Training and Development, 1986a.

Kram, K. E. "Mentoring in the Workplace." In D. T. Hall and Associates, *Career Development in Organizations*. San Francisco: Jossey-Bass, 1986b.

Kram, K. E., and Isabella, L. "Mentoring Alternatives: The Role of Peer Relationships in Career Development." *Academy of Management Journal*, 1985, *28* (1), 166.

Leschke, P. *Mentor Program Benefits New Employees: (3M) Engineering Esprit*. Minneapolis, Minn.: 3M, 1984.

Levine, H. Z. "Consensus on Career Planning." *Personnel*, 1985, *62* (3), 67–72.

Levinson, D. *Seasons of a Man's Life*. New York: Knopf, 1986.

Liles, S. "Powerful Lessons." *USA Today*, July 20, 1989, p. 2B.

McMullen, R. *Degas — His Life, Times, and Work*. Boston: Houghton Mifflin, 1984.

Management Development and Mentoring. London: PA Personnel Services, 1986.

Montagu, A. *The Natural Superiority of Women*. New York: Macmillan, 1974.

Montana, R. "Corporate Career Development Issues and Strategies." Paper presented to Bay Area Human Resource Planners, San Francisco, Nov. 1988.

Morita, A. "Education in a Changing Society." Paper presented at International Federation of Training and Development Organizations' Conference, Tokyo, Aug. 1988.

Murray-Hicks, M. *Generic Model for a Facilitated Mentoring Program*. Oakland, Calif.: MMHA, 1972.

Murray-Hicks, M. "A Behavioral Description of Mastery Performance of Professional Career Managers and of Graduate Students Entering the School of Management of John F. Kennedy University in 1976." Unpublished masters' thesis, School of Management, John F. Kennedy University, 1977.

Murray-Hicks, M. "Models, Mentors, and Mastery for Managers." Presented at the 10th Annual International Federation of Training and Development Organizations' Conference, Dublin, Ireland, 1981.

Murray-Hicks, M. "The Manager's Primer." *The Manager's Mentor*, 1987, *1* (2), 3.

Murray-Hicks, M. "It's About Time and Delegation or When Do-It-Yourself Is Doing You In." *Learning Network Magazine*, May 1990, p. 13.

Murray-Hicks, M., and Nugent, J. "Positive Motivation Process for Changing Human Behavior." Paper presented at the National Society for Performance and Instruction Conference, Rochester, N.Y., 1971.

Myers, D. W., and Humphreys, N. J. "The Caveats in Mentorship." *Business Horizons*, 1985, *28*, 9–14.

"Obituary of Dr. Benjamin Mays." *Richmond Times Dispatch*, Mar. 29, 1984, p. B2.

Odiorne, G. S. *Strategic Management of Human Resources: A Portfolio Approach*. San Francisco: Jossey-Bass, 1984.

Odiorne, G. S. *Mentoring—An American Management Innovation, Personnel Administrator*. Alexandria, Va.: American Society for Personnel Administration, 1985.

O'Reilly, L. "Mentoring Program Is Vital Part of Training." *Training Directions Forum Newsletter*, Apr. 1989, p. 4.

Orlansky, J. *The Military Value and Cost-Effectiveness of Training*. Alexandria, Va.: Institute for Defense Analyses, NATO Defense Research Section, 1989.

Pender, K. "Pac Bell's New Way to Think." *San Francisco Chronicle*, Mar. 23, 1987a, p. 1a.

Pender, K. "State PUC to Probe Pac Bell 'Krone' Training." *San Francisco Chronicle*, Mar. 24, 1987b, p. 1a.

Pender, K. "PUC Staff Assails Pac Bell Training." *San Francisco Chronicle*, June 11, 1987c, p. 1a.

Pender, K. "PUC Staff Condemns Pac Bell Training Plan." *San Francisco Chronicle*, June 11, 1987d, p. 1a.

Pender, K. "Pac Bell Reviews 'Krone' Course." *San Francisco Chronicle*, June 12, 1987e, p. 42a.

Pender, K. "Pac Bell Stops 'Kroning.'" *San Francisco Chronicle*, June 16, 1987f, p. 1a.

Phillips-Jones, L. "Establishing a Formalized Mentoring Program." *Training and Development Journal*, 1983, *37*, 38–42.

Prange, J. A., and Smalley, L. "Becoming Your Own Futurist." In *Conference Proceedings of The Nation's Workforce: Year 2000*. Milwaukee: University of Wisconsin, 1988.

Premac Associates. "Mentoring Process Works Best When It Is Kept Informal." *Research Spotlight*, June 1984, p. 55.

Reeve, C. "Helping Hands." *Chicago Tribune Magazine*, Jan. 17, 1985, pp. 8–14.

Reich, M. H. *Executive Views from Both Sides of Mentoring Personnel*. New York: American Management Association, 1985.

Robinson, S. "Mentoring Has Merit in Formal and Informal Formats." *Training Directors' Forum Newsletter*, May 1990, p. 6.

Roche, G. R. "Probing Opinions." *Harvard Business Review*, 1979, *57* (1), 15.

Rooney, Ida, Nolt and Ahern. Various sample forms. Oakland, Calif.: Rooney, Ida, Nolt and Ahern, 1989.

Shepard, Y. "A Little Help from a Mentor." *Business Month*, 1989, *134*, 15.

Spruell, G. R. "Love in the Office." *Training and Development Journal*, 1985, *39*, 21–23.

Sveiby, K. E., and Lloyd, T. *Managing Knowhow*. London: Bloomsbury, 1987.

Trudeau, G. B. "Doonesbury." *Universal Press Syndicate*, Oct. 28, 1984, p. 34.

Van Velsor, E. *Can Development Programs Make a Difference?* Greensboro, N.C.: Center for Creative Leadership, 1984.

Waldman, P. "New Agespeak." *Wall Street Journal*, July 24, 1987, *110* (18), 19.

What Makes the Difference: Success Strategies for the Promotable Woman. Dumfries, Va.: Management Training Systems, 1990.

Wilkens, M. "A Little Help from a Friend, Finding and Using a Mentor." *Pacific Bell Business Digest*, Oct. 1989, p. 2.

Zemke, R. "Using Testing Instruments in Your Training Effort." *Training/HRD*, 1982, *19*, 30–45.

Zemke, R. "Workplace Illiteracy: Shall We Overcome?" *Training*, 1989, *26* (6), 33–39.

Zey, M. G. *The Mentor Connection*. Homewood, Ill.: Dow Jones-Irwin, 1984.

Zey, M. G. "Only the Beginning: Five Major Trends That Signal the Growth of Corporate Formal Mentor Programs." In *Proceedings of the First International Conference on Mentoring*. Vol. 2.

Vancouver, B.C.: International Association for Mentoring, 1986.

Zey, M. G. "A Mentor for All Reasons." *Personnel Journal*, Jan. 1988, pp. 46–51.

Zuckerman, M. "Mentoring Has Merit in Formal and Informal Formats." *Training Directors Forum Newsletter*, May 1990, p. 6.

Index